# Stephen Hawking about the end of the world

## Discussing the central path against destruction

Cacildo Marques

ISBN: **978-1727437546**

Cover design: Cacildo Marques

Marques, Cacildo
Stephen Hawking about the end of the world/ Cacildo Marques.
Maryland, 2018.

141p.
ISBN: **978-1727437546**

1. Environment. 2. Natural Sciences. I. Title

DDC 363.05

# Stephen Hawking about the end of the world

Cacildo Marques

# CONTENTS



|   | | |
|---|---|---|
|   | Preface | viii |
| 1 | The alert | 1 |
| 2 | Ecology and warming | 9 |
| 3 | Education and attitude | 33 |
| 4 | Risks | 40 |
| 5 | Krypton and the imagination | 47 |
| 6 | Premonitions | 53 |
| 7 | Difficulties in the applications of science | 82 |
| 8 | Important physical phenomena | 86 |
| 9 | Malthusian overpopulation | 113 |

# Preface

Nobody doubts that humanity today has every chance to destroy itself, and, more than this, to destroy all life on Earth.

In addition to the risks of natural catastrophes, the risk of self-destruction has recently increased.

New world war, uncontrolled overpopulation, disregard for the environment, global warming, and mass unemployment are some ways to bring about an end, either through arrogance or through neglect.

Stephen Hawking was correct in warning on the danger and recommending the search for new planets to start over.

Many prevention mechanisms are at hand, but there seems to be no willingness to use them. Unemployment, for example, is political attitude. The public power to allow it to spread is almost the same as letting an epidemic, with a vaccine at its disposal, eliminate vulnerable populations.

Preventing the overpopulation and global warming from being pushed beyond the limits of governments is possible, but awareness of the need seems to have yet to be set.

Religious people, especially in Islam, may find that there is no problem in overcrowding with people the Earth, because the Creator has commanded, "Grow and multiply". Now, this is only part of the determination. Its complement is, "And fill the Earth". We have already fulfilled the divine request, remaining now simply to live in the deserts and Antarctica, places still inhospitable.

Underlying the whole text it is the clash between natural selection and artificial selection. Living beings have always been adapted to destruction, with some species replacing others, or acquiring new characteristics. But with artificial selection, made by the human being, the whole process is literally denatured. Nobody has any assurance that species in the world today will be able to adapt to the result of our interference, if it is not governed by the commitment to sustainability.

Before planning for a far-off future better education, better transportation, better sanitation infrastructure and better distribution of water and electricity, it precedes, with stark urgency, the responsibility to plan the means for the continuity of human life. And, as the text argues, the first provision is to follow a simple recommendation of Aristotle (see it).

Do not fall asleep without first thinking about it.

Cacildo Marques, September 2018.

## Chapter 1 - The alert

The ancients taught us that the first destruction of the world came by water, in the flood, and that the second and definitive one would come through fire. They did not take into account the fall of the giant meteor that created the Gulf of Mexico and destroyed the dinosaurs, perhaps because this story is only a hypothesis, and also because it was not known to the ancients.

In any case, the destruction of life on Earth is expected, and it will not come by water. It can come by smoke, nuclear war, or other kind of igneous activation. It certainly will not be because of forest fires, because most of the land surface is covered by oceans, which are barriers against propagation.

This fire the ancients anticipated refers to the outcome of global warming, almost certainly.

Stephen Hawking would not consider this "almost". The limit for life on Earth, he says, is only 200 more years. In addition, mankind could be extinguished in 30 years, that is, in 2047, taking into account that he made the declaration in 2017. And by that estimate, in 2217, life here will be completely extinct. On this alert he made the recommendation: the next 100 years, if we happen to have another century of existence on the planet, should be dedicated to the search for living conditions in some other world to which human specimens should be transferred.

The advice for interplanetary travel came from two Hawking convictions: first, he was betting on the possibility of conditions for human life out of the Earth's atmosphere, and second, he believed with great confidence that the point of no return to life on our planet had already been exceeded.

If he was right in the first assertion, then we must invest more and more in cosmological research and space travel. Even if we do not succeed in the search for habitable "new Earths", the knowledge accumulated in this work will certainly bring good fruit to mankind, whether or not we will have centuries of existence ahead.

If he was right about the second hypothesis, about not having more to reverse the path to the destruction of life on this blue planet, it is up to us, who are still here, to fight hard for life to last as long as possible, the best conditions we can guarantee. We all know which current instruments are available, but we should not be comfortable to use only these, once the obligation to find new means, by categorical imperative, falls on us.

**Hawking**. For many years, and until his death on March 14, 2018, in Cambridge, England, Stephen Hawking, born in Oxford, on January 8, 1942, was certainly the most popular scientist in the world. His story was portrayed still in life in a feature film, "The Theory of Everything", of 2014, an honor that Marie Curie, Pasteur, Einstein, Planck and other great names in the exact sciences had only after death. Mathematician John Nash received the Nobel Prize in Economics and also had his story told in a movie, "A Beautiful Mind", but Hawking was more famous.

Nash and Hawking had a commonality in their trajectory to make their life and their work to cause interest in the general public: both were victims of serious illness and yet they continued their research, making science advance, without letting up by the dismay that the disease normally brings to any individual. Nash, until the pharmacology brought appropriate solutions, had outbreaks of schizophrenia – in truth, persecutory disorders -, whereas Hawking, as a young man at age 21, found to be suffering from amyotrophic lateral sclerosis (ALS), a degenerative disease that in a few years transforms the individual into a dysfunctional person, unable to work. This, however, did not count for Hawking.

In his wheelchair, he continued to research and write. While having lost control of the vocal cords and fine-tuning of his fingers, he began to use a voice synthesizer, which reproduced in speech what he was writing. And the writing was first obtained with the blink of the eyes, then with the movement of the cheeks.

Doctors predicted, given the development of the disease, that he would live 50 years, but he lived 76. If he had given up his professional activities, he would have lived less than the 50 that had been predicted. He was married twice and when died he left three children.

In 1979 he took up the Lucasian Chair of Mathematics at Cambridge University, working there until his retirement in 2009. The chair is named Lucasian because it was founded in 1663 by parliamentarian Henry Lucas, representative of that university in the English Parliament. By his own determination, the chair occupant would have to teach two math classes per week and be available for at least two hours a week to clear the students' questions. The first holder of the chair was Professor Isaac Barrow, and the second was his syllabus, Isaac Newton. As Newton's chair, when a teacher is inducted into it already receives special treatment within academia and also the press. Historically, Hawking was among those who most honored this distinction. It was succeeded in 2009 by Michael Green, who was succeeded in 2015 also by a syllabus, Michael Cates.

Among Hawking's many contributions to science are the Hawking-Penrose Singularity Theorems and Hawking Radiation. The singularity relates to the concept of gravitation given by Albert Einstein's Theory of General Relativity. By this theory, gravity results from a curvature in space-time caused by the presence of matter or energy. According to Karl Schwarzshild, a German physicist, a singularity occurs when the ratio between mass and volume of a substance exceeds a certain value, which gives rise to a point of infinite density and energy. Around this point, a field is formed where the curvature of space-time is also infinite, attracting objects in such a way that even light cannot escape. In this way, the phenomenon became known as a "black hole". From 1970, Hawking and Roger Penrose investigated Einstein's equations on the curvature of space-time and found outlets to apply them to all kinds of objects, while making them describe the black holes from the parameters electric charge, rotation and mass. Applying these solutions at the birth of the universe, Hawking showed that we would have the "initial singularity" of infinite energy and density that would have spawned the Big Bang.

While using his deep knowledge in Relativity and Quantum, the scientist speculated on the possibility of time travel and to regions located light-years away. These, in theory, may occur through "wormholes", which are tunnels of almost infinitesimal thickness that form in the quantum world at greatly reduced intervals of time. They connect our environment with seemingly inaccessible places and epochs of space-time, and if science provides a suitable means of widening its width or shrinking the size of the traveler, then we can transit through them. It may be imagined, even without endorsement of Hawking, that although Sigmund Freud has rejected the possibility of premonition throughout his life, the capacity of the unconscious, according to Freud himself, to see through the walls may contain the key to visions of future, which, even nebulae, some persons have, and can also explain the feeling of *dejá vu*, which almost every human being experiences.

In relation to journeys to the past, Hawking respected the "paradox of the grandfather", or "paradox of the mad scientist", the one who, traveling for decades, shot and killed his grandfather at point-blank range, which would make him impossible to exist, once he could not have been born. Without a visible solution to circumvent such an obstacle, Hawking invited us to think of the possibility of travel to the future, at least. Obviously, if we ever get to go to the past, it is almost certain that something will hinder our ability to intervene there. Thus, if travelers of the future are circulating among us, they walk around here as observers, with no chance of preventing Andrew from marrying Lucia or of enabling a third quadrennial term followed by a current president of the United States.

Hawking saw yet another two theoretical possibilities for time travel. One of them was to make a spacecraft into the orbit of a black hole, with which time would pass at much greater speed than normal. This attempt is discarded in practice, because there would be no volunteer one to approach a black hole. The other is to travel at a speed close to that of light, which is just under $3*10^8$ m/s, or 300,000 km/s. By the Theory of Relativity, this causes the passage of time to change. With a ship 2,000,000 times faster than Apollo X, four years after takeoff we would be traveling through time.

The other major contribution of the scientist, the Hawking Radiation, belongs to the area of Quantum Mechanics. In the case of tiny particles, empty space-time is empty only apparently, since, according to Hawking, there is a permanent onslaught between virtual particle and virtual antiparticle, elements that are formed and then annihilate, when found. When these pairs of particles form near the event horizon of a black hole, so that one of the particles is captured and another one escapes, then the one that is captured carries negative mass or energy, causing the black hole to lose mass or energy, in accordance with conservation laws. Thus, this particle that escaped represents a portion of dissolution of the black hole, which "evaporates" in the form of radiation. This was called Hawking Radiation.

*Physicist Stephen Wawking*

One of Hawking's latest works, developed in partnership with his collaborator Thomas Hertog, investigates the existence of multiple universes, the multiverse, postulating that eternal expansion occurs in the universe we inhabit and in other parallel universes, but not in the larger universe within the universe where multiple universes exist, after being generated in the Big Bang. The formulation is based on String Theory, branch of Physics that seeks to reconcile Theory of Relativity and Quantum Mechanics, while describing the fundamental elements of the Universe as small vibratory strings, instead of simple particles.

In addition to his important research and formulation in Physics, Hawking devoted himself to writing scientific papers of disclosure, which has increased his fame among readers worldwide. Among the books published for this purpose, the best known are "A Brief History of Time", "The Grand Design", "The Universe in a Nutshell", "A Briefer History of Time", and "On the Shoulders of Giants".

**Fictions**. It is important to note that throughout the 20th century, until at least 1969, when three men descended on the surface of the Moon, interest in science was aroused in young people by science fiction texts in almost all cases, and that today this role has been transferred to dissemination texts in the essay format. Jules Verne's "Journey to the Moon", which moved the imagination of readers alike, was concretely realized in 1969, while bringing the fiction of space journeys into the universe of total likelihood, except for a certain number of victims of the conspiracy theory and another portion of illiterates, who do not "swallow" that deed. The case of the illiterate is easy to understand, because they, with rare exceptions, live in the environment of the palpable, and what they see at a distance can only be absorbed as something very close, so that the moon resembles a mozzarella pizza, in its size, and the sun to a shiny car wheel shell, with nothing outside the Earth's surface, except meteorites and hailstones, are objects of more than two dimensions. The reader should not think that the illiterate has some guilt for thinking this way or for being illiterate. It is the fault of the political system in which he lives, for there are few faults more culpable than to keep a teenager without reading and writing.

As for believers in conspiracy theory, they are not victims of the absence of first letter teaching, but they fall prey to the educational system anyway. Just as the illiterate cannot conceive astronomical distances and perspectives, the adept of conspiracy theory does not assimilate the idea of the essential equality of human beings, especially in their fragility. He imagines that among us there is an organized team of supermen who, while being susceptible to influenza and having to satisfy basic physiological needs, are endowed with a malicious power and deep knowledge that allows them to manipulate and control the rest of the individuals, who are similar to each other, but not to them. He believes in a secret caste, whose members roam the streets as if they were ordinary people, but of ordinary people only have the outward appearance and some behaviors that allow them to disguise their special nature. Essential equality comes from the Abrahamic religions, but also from Zen Buddhism and other doctrines. If that is not enough, the young man has yet to study John Locke's concept of "tabula rasa" in high school. If the "tabula rasa" is not the white slate that Locke imagined in the seventeenth century, and it is not, as Steven Pinker asserts, the concept does not cancel out, because biology puts us all in a unique condition, as it also puts, in their own reality, horses, tunas, eagles and mosquitoes. To this day, the only dowry that can give more power to some than other ones, outside open political conventions, is the patent, whether registered or not, derived from objects of intellectual creation. Imagine the owner of a fleet of trucks that develops a cheap air-powered engine. It can register and advertise the product, enjoying the 20 years of rights over it, but can also keep it in his vehicles only, gaining a huge advantage over competitors, who have to continue to spend on fuel. His drivers may know the system, and receive a tip not to reveal it, or they may be kept in ignorance with some gimmick. It is, therefore, the patent, of product or scheme, that can allow an individual to overlap with others, in economic and even political power. The heirs will need a lot of perspicacity so as not to be dragged into the gales of creative destruction. The alternative to this, the condition of birth in higher castes, is a thing of antiquity, which today remains in some societies as an uncomfortable fossil. In India, for decades, the caste system has lost its official character, as has also been the case with South Africa's apartheid. If caste cultures remain, it is because certain millennial traditions take a long time to be extinguished. But the actual disappearance of the model is inexorable, because the Republican system, with short mandates of democratically elected rulers, is incompatible with it in the long run.

In the same way that with the dream, which is almost always articulated in the brain of the sleeping individual as a kind of fictional story, in the brain of the man afflicted with conspiracy theory the arrangement happens as a case of fiction, without his realizing it, just like in the dream. The big difference is that now the process is sickening, and progressive. The believer of the "theory" despairs of the difficulty of convincing the healthy people of the pretended truth that he sees. And just as an alcoholic dependent counteracts the friends' diagnosis on his problem, the conspiration believer is deeply troubled when someone tries to disassemble his "thesis", and may even activate an adrenaline rush, which causes him to spend hours in the changed state.

The delusional disorder of the persecutory type, the old mania of persecution, acts in diverse way, according to the information that the individual owns. In someone who is minimally politicized, for good or evil, the "I", the object of persecution, is replaced by "we".

Whether this individual acquires power, whether political or economic, and is at an advanced stage of inculcation, the risks of him embarking on violent paths in the search for a solution to what he sees as the problem of the world are enormous. The most notorious victim of belief in conspiracy theory was undoubtedly Adolf Hitler. All others, including Nero, produced minor damage.

## Chapter 2 - Ecology and warming

**Ecology**. The year 1969 not only meant a change of vision in relation to science fiction texts, but brought with the trip to the Moon the sudden awareness that the Earth, seen from space as a little blue acorn, is a fragile being that demands our care, and that can be destroyed or desertified by our actions, if they are not responsible. From one moment to the next the development of Ecology, a branch of Biology that did not seem to be so necessary, took hold.

By definition, Ecology is the scientific area that studies the relationships of living beings with each other and with the environment in which they live, that is, the environment of their neighborhood. The term is formed by the Greek words *oíkos* (house) + *logos* (speech). As part of this study, concepts such as ecosystem, biome, food chain, biodiversity and sustainability were developed. In the latter term, sustainability, it is understood to be the key to the healthy prolongation of life on Earth. Development may be predatory or sustainable, and one or the other depends on the attitudes of the human species.

The Age of the Discoveries, concomitant with the cultural movement of the Renaissance, and the Industrial Revolution, about four centuries later, were the two great outpourings of progress that humankind lived after the European Middle Ages. It was still the era of innocence, in the sense that we thought that natural resources were elastic, endless, and self-regenerating. The disappearance of some animal species used in food, such as auroque and doudo, was not enough to wake people up about the destructive capacity of the human element over the surrounding nature. The first voyage of circumnavigation of the Earth undertaken by Fernao de Magalhaes between 1520 and 1522 (having crossed the Pacific Ocean, he died on reaching the Philippines, struck by an arrow in 1521, and his men continued the expedition) did nothing to shake the conviction that we were lords of the world, and that it would gladly serve us in all future ages, until Our Lord, the Lord of lords, came and performed the final judgment here a few millennia ahead. It should be noted that the first destruction, that of the Flood, was caused by the iniquity of the men of the time, which led the Lord to plan a renewal from a righteous man named Noah. The same persons who believe in this report imagined that the second and final destruction, which will only leave ashes, will come by the omnipotent will of the Creator, without us, children of Adam, having any part in anticipating or postponing this tragic occurrence.

What we will discuss in this work is the possibility of escaping this guilt by anticipation. If we control our interference to the point where we let life on Earth run its course without compromising ecological equilibrium in an incorrigible way, we may counter the Hawking's prognosis. Do we still have that chance?

**Industry**. With the Industrial Revolution, the acts of related externalities, of opening roads, overturning forests, polluting rivers, and dumping soot around the factories only widened the illusion that we humans could arrogantly control nature in our favor without ever having a negative response from it.

Earlier, with the inventions of Archimedes and the members of the School of Mechanics of Alexandria, such as Aristarchus of Samos, Ctesibius, Hero, Hipparchus, Claudius Ptolemy and others, not forgetting the extraordinary figures of geometer Euclid of Alexandria and librarian Eratosthenes of Cyrene, coming later to the name of the not less remarkable Hypacia, woman died by fanatics catholic religious in the year 415, in date that corresponds today to 8 of March, present day of the women, already with the inventions and concepts developed by these sages over the centuries, man began to strengthen his conviction that he could dispose of nature in an irresponsible way, aware that it is there to serve us.

However, from those Alexandrian times, from the third century BC until the nineteenth century, with the consolidation of the Industrial Revolution, our intervention in ecological diversity was small, provided by instruments such as plow, sickle, lever, gunpowder and arquebus. One has only to compare the felling of the trees of a farm at the expense of ax and sickle with what a chainsaw came to provide and we will see a sample of the power difference between the medieval man, the Renaissance man and us. Moving forward in science and technology, we arrive at the locomotive, the steamboat, the hydroelectric plant, the radio, the airplane, the TV, the nuclear submarine, the atomic bomb, the Internet and the cell phone, which today is a small pocket computer. A given calculation of determinants (of order 20) that at the end of the nineteenth century was estimated to be realized in a hundred years is now done in a few seconds with the use of basic computers. If we still do not step on Mars, we already sent a probe to photograph Pluto closely, in the fringes of the Solar System. And we have space telescopes photographing for us other galaxies, far beyond our Milky Way.

This difference in calculation time, from one hundred years to two or three seconds, is a sample of how our power of intervention in nature has multiplied over the last two centuries, and especially in the twentieth century.

Those whom the press inappropriately calls "climate skeptics", who only intend to be skeptics, since they are simply refractory, imagine that we would only produce a destructive intervention in the life of the Earth if at the same time we exploded a great arsenal of atomic bombs in the several continents of the globe and that all the rest of human activities based on modern technologies only tickle the Earth's surface. When the data on the melting of the polar ice caps is presented to them, they immediately respond with data from the low temperatures in the winter, without realizing that the melting of the ice is behind this increase of amplitude of the thermal scale, both for more and for less.

Climate skeptics are all of us who discuss the various forms of human intervention, whether involuntary or not, in the climatic and ecological balance of the planet. Because we do not yet know the dimensions of this new reality, and we bet, almost all the time, on the possibility of seeing much less damage than what has already occurred.

The refractories are those who radically deny the anthropogenic warming, while building an immense barrier ahead of themselves to prevent the intellection of any information related to the possibility of human intervention in the Earth's climate. Many of these are capable scientists who could contribute to finding solutions. By rejecting the existence of the problem, they act only as flamethrowers, magnifying the possible damages.

Refractories are nothing new in science. In Ancient Greece, through the accounts of Aristotle, Zeno of Elea presented paradoxes to question the explanations of mathematicians of the pre-Socratic period. The attitude was positive because, far from hampering the progress of the research, it helped to find ways to get around the obstacle. If they could not absorb the paradox in theory, it was because it was incomplete or inconsistent. The most notorious case was the oxymoron called "Achilles and the tortoise", to check the theories of motion. From the image created by Zeno, Achilles bet on the tortoise, and as he was known to be faster than it, gave it an advantage. It would go a few leagues ahead. At one point, Achilles would have overcome that advantage he gave, reaching the tortoise's starting point. But at that very moment, the tortoise, even with its slowness, would have run the other way too. When Achilles arrived at this new place, it would already be at a third point, and so on. Repeating that reasoning, Achilles would not reach the turtle, because it would always be ahead.

As we know, only from the Renaissance, with the work of Galileo and Huygens, is that the studies of the movement could respond to that and other aporias of antiquity.

**Refractory**. In the early twentieth century Jules-Henri Poincaré wrote: "Lord Kelvin is the most refractory scientist I know." He tells that Kelvin had news on the experience of Santos Dumont at Bagatelle Field on November 12, 1906, making to lift up a tool heavier than air. This was done from the discovery of the Brazilian engineer regarding the vertical propulsion of the engines, when he was using the engine to perform the aerial maneuvers of his Balloon 14. William Thompson, Lord Kelvin, president of the Royal Society that days, certainly did not receive information about the discovery, once, according to Poincaré, he made a point of publishing in English newspaper an article "demonstrating" that flight of heavier than air was a technical impossibility. He stated, "Heavier than air flying machines are impossible", while expressing his faith in balloons. He had interpreted the news of the November 12 flight as a "fake news".

The climate refractories are, therefore, in good company, even though when they present themselves as "skeptics" they are forming a line with the pasty, obscure side of the deceivers. In addition, Kelvin was refractory, but not an enemy of the evidence. He died a year after that first takeoff, and it was a pity he did not live to see the planes being used, on the proposal of Santos Dumont to the French government, to fight Germans and Turks in World War I. Here is another parenthesis in favor of Kelvin. A scientist, anyone, can be deceived by a regular newspaper news, a not-specialized publication, or by news of electronic organs. That's because in these cases the news is always incomplete. If the news of a new invention comes, it is hardly accompanied by the scientific discovery that has generated it. The difference between a new invention and a new utility model is that in the first there must always be a scientific novelty involved.

Someone reporting, at the beginning of the 20$^{th}$ century, that a researcher was able to fly in a machine heavier than air, without explaining how, it is almost the same as releasing today the news that a scientist has managed to make a trip to the past, in the flesh, with the possibility of interfering there. We can write an article, using the paradox of the grandfather, demonstrating that the news is a liar.

Without the Santos Dumont's discovery of vertical propulsion, there was no way anyone could understand the flight he carried out in Paris. And he knew so much about the novelty of the situation that he had summoned the press to witness the experiment. The reporters saw, but could not expose what was behind.

Refractories of the present are of a more disturbing nature, because, in addition to clusters of resistance, they do not contribute to the scientific advance, at least in the aspects in which they are extreme unbelievers.

Science, in order to advance, needs critic persons, within the scientific activity itself, who scrutinize the statements of other researchers. Every discovery and every thesis must be subject to refutation, as Karl Popper put it, following the line of Bertrand Russell's skepticism. The refutation process should not be in the hands of refractory, sabotaging or lazy, of those who have not read and disliked. It is a noble activity, of people who are dedicated to verify if there are flaws in the reasoning, the data or the conclusions of those who present a scientific novelty. This task was most striking, for example, in the nearly three centuries in which mathematicians sought to solve Fermat's Problem, which was to demonstrate that the basis of a Pythagorean triple - first cathetus, second cathetus, and hypotenuse – when the exponent of the first relation of Trigonometry, with the square of the hypotenuse, $a^2$, equating to the sum of the squares of the legs, $b^2 + c^2$, is replaced by any integer greater than 2, the original exponent of the terms of equality, cannot be simultaneously whole. Whenever someone presented a supposed solution, immediately mathematicians from various parts of the world began to check the work, always finding some flaw. The biggest reason was that there were huge prizes, offered by big universities and even governments, to the lucky man who would reach the solution. Finally, in 1995, Andrew John Wiles, a mathematician born in Cambridge, England, in 1953, published his definitive proof, without fail, two years after having brought to light a first version that soon was disassembled by the critics.

This work of refutation in the twentieth and twenty-first centuries is fundamental because humanity has long been deceived in the name of science in earlier times, all in the best of good faith. One example was the technique of bleeding, which Medicine used for centuries until the mid-nineteenth century. The process consisted in extracting a large amount of blood from the patient's body, in the hope that the disease that affected him would flow along the portion taken from the blood. A large number of patients were hastened to death by this method, as were the cases, for example, of Ada Lovelace, creator of the computer programming language, and her father, the poet Lord Byron, but this did not convince physicians that the procedure was wrong. Nowadays, if someone comes up with a new method of cure that has not been subjected to refutability, he soon becomes seen as very suspicious and, as a rule, has his novelty discarded from the academic circles until the second order.

The term "refutability" is very strong, and it gives the impression that scientific work is rejected beforehand. In fact, that's almost it. An important cause-and-effect relationship discovered today, however spectacular, needs to be replicated. If a laboratory in Australia has achieved the feat in primacy, another in France, Japan or the United States needs to achieve the same result, under identical conditions. Otherwise, the communication is only hypothesized, if it is not refuted soon.

So how is it possible to develop works on Cosmology if we are not there in the other galaxies testing facts? The task, as Einstein has always emphasized, is primarily mathematical. Currently artificial satellites help researchers by photographing and sending to Earth all that is before them, but most of the time the images arrive to confirm calculations and equations. Some novelty appears in the photographs, leading to new speculations, but no assurance would be given to the behavior of stars and nebulae if we did not have mathematics as the mainstay for the research.

When Einstein stated that whatever "your mathematical difficulty" was, his was "much greater", he did not mean that he faced difficulty at any point in basic Mathematics, but that for his work it was necessary to use very advanced resources, before which anyone would be in trouble.

When the academia institutes a particular view of the stage of research in the "hard" sciences as mainstream, it is inescapably supported by mathematical results. Refractories, if they want to evolve into skeptics, already know what to do: checking numbers, equations, theorems, and models thoroughly for some inconsistency. Despite the disappointment they will have with their creations, the scientists responsible for the dethroned idea will only have to thank. And critics will gain recognition for having prevented an error from spreading. Without this attitude of scrutiny, the negationists are aligned not with the skeptics, but with the adherents of some conspiracy theory.

**Heating**. From 1952 onwards, the press began to deal sparingly with the theme of "climate change". A November 1957 report in *The Hammond Times*, Indiana, USA, opened to the general public one of the research objects of Professor Roger Revelle, of the University of California at San Diego, which was precisely the question of human action on climate. Here the researcher described the rise in temperature on Earth caused by $CO_2$ emissions, the carbon dioxide, in the form of what he called the "greenhouse effect". The concept of the greenhouse effect, however, is not from the twentieth century, but from the previous century, formulated by Svante August Arrhenius, who won the Nobel Prize for Chemistry in 1903, and greenhouse gases go beyond carbon dioxide, once they can be also nitrogen oxide, methane and others.

Those who resist the idea of the power of human action on the global climate argue that the observed warming would have to occur even if no human individual were on Earth. In a millennium or another, changes in the planet's temperature occur, they say. Basic school textbooks tell us that we Americans came from Asia between seven thousand and eleven thousand years ago crossing the Behring Strait in freezing times of the region. They think that if the strait was frozen millennia ago and is not now, then these thaws visit us from time to time, without us being able to interfere. Now, we came on ice is not much likely. That we came by the strait is almost one hundred percent true fact. Researchers, incidentally, have already shown that many millennia ago fishermen could travel on their vessels for long distances at sea. It is more likely that there were more islands in the area of the strait, islands now covered by the waters. Thus, the passage from one island to another, until the arrival to the American continent was very facilitated. Yes, 21,000 years ago Asia and America were connected. But the last glaciation, at that time, led to the current conformation. If we made the crossing ten thousand years later, it was not walking or skiing on the ice. We came, almost certainly, by water path.

Skeptics, who are the most knowledgeable scientists, know of current global warming and attribute its cause, based on very strong evidence, to human action. Refractories accept that current global warming exists, but without having any idea what its cause might be, they deny the anthropogenic cause. For them, the reason must be somewhere in the interior of the planet, in outer space, in the ionosphere, or in our own atmosphere, without us being able to identify it today and without perhaps having a chance to identify it in the future.

This attitude is still a position, but it is similar to that of those bishops who refused to look at the telescope that Galileo Galilei wanted them to see, keeping their convictions unshaken and trying to obtain the prison sentence for the scientist of Padua.

It is important to note that the negationist position is of isolated individuals, although there are some of them who hold research positions in scientific institutions. As for the research centers in the climate area, there is no important body in the world defending a refractory position.

Projections indicate that throughout the $21^{st}$ century the average temperature will increase up to 4.8%. If all reasonable steps are taken to reduce the rate of warming, there will still be an increase of at least 0.3%. This latter scenario is auspicious, but it is almost entirely improbable.

In addition to the increase in average temperature, which should be higher on the surface of the soil than in the oceans, it is expected an increase of the sea level - small, not the rise of half a meter or a meter as the alarmists spread there -, increase of the melting polar ice caps, droughts, snowstorms and changes in the rainfall levels. There may also be a disappearance of species and a problem in the food supply, because of the greater frequency of floods.

Volcanic eruptions, solar radiation and variations in the Earth's orbit are natural possibilities for climate change. Before our industrial activities became large enough to interfere with the global climate, these were the options that were taken into account to account for major changes in the heating or cooling of the Earth's surface. From the mid-twentieth century, and in increasing proportion, the facts are no longer so simple. Not only did we install a large number of artificial satellites around our planet but also we have produced harmful effects as a result of externalities linked to most of our performances within the contemporary way of life.

Previously, it used to be a train carrying hundreds of people driven by a locomotive that smoked in the air. Also the steamer emitted its smoke. If that changed the temperature of the environment miles away, it was at an imperceptible level. Now there are millions, almost one billion, of families that own their own car and traffic in it almost every day pouring $CO_2$ into the environment.

This, in addition to transforming the Earth's atmosphere into a giant spherical furnace, by the greenhouse effect, brings the additional problem of prolonging the high temperature. Even if we can stop all sources of gas emissions and reheating, the already set up situation prevents short-term cooling. By the greenhouse effect itself, the return to the status quo, at the temperature prior to global warming, would require decades or centuries.

A five-day blockade promoted by truck drivers on Brazilian highways between May 21 and 26, 2018, led to fuel shortages in large cities. With the sharp reduction in car traffic, air pollution in the city of Sao Paulo, the largest in South America, fell by half compared to normal working days. No one wants to be forced to leave his car in the garage, but we want society returns, by consensual means and with the help of science, to this degree of pollution, that is, if not yet the ideal, something very desirable.

When Blaise Pascal launched his collective transportation proposal in seventeenth-century Paris, his intention was for the poor to have access to the carriage, a collective carriage, anticipating that there would not be a day when each family owned its private car. If today each family has its car in the more developed countries, as in the United States (although with the advent of Reaganomics — concessions of public services - many black families have fallen into impoverishment and were left without their vehicle, as seen in the Hurricane Katrina disaster in New Orleans), this is due more to an industry insistence, since Henry Ford, than to an individual need to abandon train, bus and other vehicles of collective transportation. Let us not, however, want to blame Ford and other industrialists of the early twentieth century, for they could not imagine that their product was one of the main culprits of the turn, that is, by the time when human actions would interfere with the global climate.

Henry Ford died in 1947 and global warming became a concern in the mid-1950s. Other industrialists were in the race for more heating products, such as the car plant competitors, aircraft manufacturers, motorcycles, ship producers and so on. Everyone was sure that if they harm the environment, it would be in strictly local level.

From what we know of thermodynamics, since the time of the French Revolution, the dissipation of energy, which occurs in the form of heat, is almost always pure loss. If we light a filament lamp, part of the electric energy spent there turns into luminous energy, which we want, while another part dissipates as heat. What until the 1940s was understood as mere loss, a mere waste of energy, is now seen as a harmful by-product contributing to global warming in contact with greenhouse gases.

The human ingenuity can find solutions that we do not see at the moment. In the case of light bulbs, in 1962 General Electric introduced the *Light Emitting Diode* (LED) lamp, which today has great popularity. Since the beginning of the 21$^{st}$ century dichroic lamps (Greek *dichroos* = bicolor) have spread in the market, because of their low cost of consumption, but they give off heat in a great proportion, although not as much as the old filament lamps. Already the LED lamps dissipate heat in tiny quantity.

For car engines and other vehicles, the trend, not only for the advancement of technology, but for the very awareness of sustainability, triggered in the Rio-92 Conference, is to replace the use of fossil fuels such as gasoline and oil by means of cleaner means, from biofuels to the use of electricity and hydrogen. It will come as no surprise if solar-powered vehicles fill the streets in a few years. But in all of these alternative alternatives to coal and oil, although the main concern is the reduction of greenhouse gas emissions, research needs to focus attention on the reduction of heat dissipation, which automatically means an increase in the efficiency of the machines.

Of course, we must be prepared to face setbacks, such as President Donald John Trump's decision to reject the Paris Climate Agreement. At his whim, the most palpable result of his policy was the resurrection of the price of a barrel of oil in the first half of 2018. Had the compromise been validated, with the fulfillment of the Agreement by all major industrial powers, the price of oil would have been maintained in a downward curve, until the global abandonment of this type of energy, predicted for the decade of 2030.

In the presidential system, the president has excessive power. The world now needs to make sure the next US ruler has a position different from that of Donald Trump regarding climate risk, whether he is of the Republican Party or the Democratic Party. This misunderstanding by part of the president, along with others of the same level, will cost him recognition for his positive policies, as in the case of the struggle to establish full employment. Anthropogenic warming refractories, as seems to be the case with Trump, are a small minority among upper-level people, so it will be an unlikely event if his successor is an adherent of the same belief. If there are two doubles of quadrennial terms, completing 16 years, of rejection of climate agreements by the United States, then Hawking's prognosis will greatly increase its chance of being correct, not because one among more than two hundred countries acts as a rebel, but because this rebellious country is the most powerful and most industrialized on Earth.

It is also disturbing the possibility that China may evade its own signature, which in early 2018 abandoned the path to modern democracy when it restored the status of presidential re-election indefinitely. A possible prolonged world war being as a central actor a country of 1.35 billion inhabitants, almost 20% of the global population, will not leave a living soul among the members of the human species, and that is why the world is going to take revenge for presidential vitality according to its recent constitutional reform. Shortly after the end of World War II, the United States tried to limit the maximum period for a ruler in two quadrennial terms. The states of Europe gradually reduced the size of their mandates, such as France, which, under the Sarkozy presidency, reduced the period from seven to five years, limiting in two five-year terms the possibility of presidential exercise by one person. And the European Union, by instituting the presidency of the European Council, limited its exercise in two 2.5-year terms. China, therefore, acted against history, heading back to the days of Hitler, Franco, Papa Doc, Somoza and Ferdinand Marcos, these latter ones being stubble from the period between the wars or the immediate postwar period.

The UN was created, replacing the failed and ephemeral League of Nations, to ensure peace between the member countries. This means that, even though there is no explicit purpose of undermining lifelong dictatorships, this work is embedded in the work of the entity, which knows from its decades-long experience that spending on its Peacekeeping Troops occurs in areas where anti-democratic governments flourish. In recent times it is also involved with ensuring the health of the climate, as it could not be otherwise.

**Measures**. An important step in the history of environmental action came on March 21, 1994, when the United Nations Framework Convention on Climate Change, based in Bonn, Germany, came into force, after it was officialized on 9 May 1992.

Prior to this, the UNEP, United Nations Environment Program, with headquarter in Nairobi, Kenya, had been established in 1972 to help developing countries adopt sound practices with acceptable ecological standards. This body emerged as a result of the United Nations Conference on the Environment in Stockholm, Sweden, in June of that year.

The performance of these organs, however, had been very discreet and ineffective. In 1988, the Intergovernmental Panel on Climate Change (IPCC), a World Meteorological Organization (WMO) partnership with the UNEP. The IPCC web page is *www.ipcc.ch*

The validity of the Panel's creation is unquestionable and one proof of this is that on October 12, 2007, its group of scientists, led by Indian industrial engineer Rajendra Pachauri, shared the Nobel Peace Prize with Al Gore Jr., the environmental activist who, after being vice president, was candidate to the presidency of the United States by the Democratic Party in year 2000 and is cousin of the writer Gore Vidal. Since 2007, there is no well-informed person in the world who ignores the IPCC's actions. The part that went to the Panel's prize money was split among the team's researching members.

The IPCC has issued a series of Climate Assessment Reports, the first one (FAR: First Assessment Report) being that of 1990 and, because of it, the UN General Assembly decided to create the Convention on Climate Change, which came into force in 1994, as we have seen above.

In Rio-92, the Earth Summit, a Complementary Report was issued.

The Second Assessment Report (SAR) was published in 1995

and served as the basis for the Kyoto Protocol, finalized in 1998 and put into force in 2004, when the Russia's accession was achieved. Under this Protocol, the signatory countries committed themselves to taking measures to reduce the emission of the following greenhouse gases: carbon dioxide ($CO_2$), methane ($CH_4$), nitrous oxide ($N_2O$), sulfur hexafluoride ($AF_6$), hydrofluorocarbons (HFC's) and perfluorocarbons (PFC's).

The Third Assessment Report (TAR) came to light in 2001 and saw the need to broaden the group of countries that signed the Kyoto Protocol and also to draft a more restrictive protocol to come into force after expiry, in 2012, of that which was in force.

The Fourth Assessment Report (AR4) was published in 2003, with an indication that it would be completed in 2007. That year, an agreement was reached in Bali, Indonesia, whereby developing countries would invest in renewable energy, in gradual substitution to the fossil fuels, with a view to stagnating the increase in global warming.

The Fifth Assessment Report (AR5) came out in 2014. It deepens the certainty about human action on global warming, raising from 90% the degree established in 2007 ("very possible") to 95% ("extremely possible ").

It is clear, therefore, that even for the IPCC, the skeptical position is valid: there is still a margin of 5% of possibility that the majority is wrong in relation to the bet on anthropogenic heating, since it is not the solution of an mathematical equation, with variables isolated from any strange disturbance. Refractories, on the other hand, embrace with certainty the complementary understanding, that, if there is any chance for human participation in warming, this is only 5%, if at all, this if they really admit some controversy. We know that an extreme refractory puts this rate at 0%.

If they are really skeptical, and not absolutely refractory, the negationists of the anthropogenic action must adopt the prudent attitude that the theory of games in its incipient form recommends. While returning to this French scientist-philosopher, the famous Pascal's Bet, which he presented in note 233, section III, of his book Thoughts, consists of a scheme that inaugurated the reasoning of

Mathematical Expectation. If you believe in divinity, i. e., if you accept the transcendence of the soul, acting in conformity with that belief, and transcendence exists in fact, you will have an infinite gain after death; if you believe and it does not exist, you will have finite loss (a life); if you do not believe and it exists, you will have infinite loss; if you do not believe and it does not exist, you will have finite gain (a life). If it is in your hands to choose between believing or disbelieving, the expected value, or the mathematical expectation, of choosing to believe is always greater than or equal to choosing to disbelieve.

Let us now make an adaptation of Pascal's Bet for the case of global warming. The individual is now represented by the human species. Suppose that the disappearance of life on Earth in the next 100 years will come as a consequence of global warming only, with this invitation being given to IPCC supporters and refractories, according to which warming exists without the human hand having any responsibility for the fact. If warming is anthropogenic (H) and humanity believes (A) in this, acting to reverse the picture, it will gain thousands of years of life on the planet, for example, over 100,000 years. If it is false that warming has anthropogenic origin (~H), mankind will have finite loss of useless investment for 100 years. If mankind does not believe (~B) and the warming is anthropogenic, it will lose 100,000 years, whereas it will have a gain of 100 years, for not investing in something wrong, if the cause of the warming is not human action (~B).

|  | Anthropogenic (H) | Not anthropogenic (~H) |
|---|---|---|
| Believing (B) | +100,000 years | -100 years |
| Not believing (~B) | -100,000 years | +100 years |

The above table shows that regardless of whether the global warming that the measurements have recorded is a result of human action or not, the bet on not believing (~B) is the choice of the losing side.

Even reversing the value of the probability considered by the IPCC, giving 5% for the anthropogenic case and 95% for nonhuman interference, the person who believes is gaining. Multiplying 100,000 years by the probability 0.5 we will have 5,000 years, while multiplying -100 years by the probability 0.95 we will have -95 years. The sum, which is the mathematical expectation of he who believe, gives 4,905 years. For those who do not believe, we multiplied -100,000 by 0.5 to get -5,000, and we multiplied 100 by 0.95 to get 95 years. The sum of -5,000 with +95 results -4.905, which is the mathematical expectation of not believing.

If we lower the absolute value in the first number column from 100,000 to 10,000 and re-calculate the accounts with the same probabilities of the previous calculation, even so those who believe will be at an advantage from 405 years to -405 years from unbelievers. As the absolute value in column H will always be greater than or equal to that written in the ~H column, the gain of those who believe will never be less than that of those who disbelieve, as already verified by Pascal.

The negationist may argue that the premise of the disappearance of life as a consequence of warming is meaningless because, in his belief, this warming is the result of nature's action, which will know how, as in previous times, reverse the temperature growth curve in the right moment. Now, when a great earthquake occurs, involving large cities, many pray, many cry, saying that nature will know how to take care of saving the lives of their children. However, it does not have that kind of commitment. Even for the deity, we can be nothing more than tiny, laborious little ants that the flood kills and carries in a matter of minutes at the start of the storms. Such an assertion is not intended to ridicule the bet of this negationist who did not accept the premise above, but merely to remember that his argument is just another bet, which may be too optimistic.

Of course, many research centers are looking for solutions to minimize the escalation of global warming.

In Spain, for example, the CSIC, Superior Council for Scientific Research, has produced a series of recommendations for people and governments in the precautionary approach to climate change.

> 1 - *Transportation*. Reduce car use and travel more by collective transportation.

2 - *Home*. Prefer devices with less energy consume and turn off those that are not in use.

3 - *Waste*. Get used to separating the garbage, supporting the recycling.

4 - *Materials*. Reuse as much as possible.

5 - *Water*. Decrease consumption.

6 - *Irrigation*. Irrigate the garden plants to a minimum and give preference to the drip system.

7 - *Urbanization*. Prefer places where water is guaranteed for the long term.

8 - *Nature*. Minimize environmental impacts.

9 - *Constructions*. Build homes with good thermal insulation.

10 - *Crevice*. Improve insulation on doors and windows to let less heat escape.

11 - *Sun*. Invest in photovoltaic panels providing leftover power to the grid.

12 - *Alternatives*. Value alternative energies so they are cheaper.

13 - *Taxes*. Embed fiscal incentives for resource conservation.

14 - *Soil*. Minimize changes in land use.

15 - *Impact*. Give greater importance to environmental impact analyzes.

16 - *Species*. Avoid transporting them out of their natural habitat.

17 - *Invaders*. Do not release into the environment animals that may represent invasive species.

18 - *Chemistry*. Reduce the use of chemical compounds such as antibiotics, fertilizers and aerosols.

19 - *Education*. Educate children about the value of ecosystems.

20 - *Governments*. Require long-term sustainable management of the various natural resources.

**Amazon**. The Amazon rainforest has been destroyed day after day. From 1499, when Amerigo Vespucci discovered the mouth of the Amazon River, until 1960, the year of the inauguration of Brasilia, the devastation had been of little importance, and we can say that it was a sustainable occupation. With the rise of rubber-related businesses for automobile tires at the beginning of the 20th century, the city of Manaus, capital of the State of Amazonas, experienced a period of glory, and a railroad was built further south, in the territory of Guapore, now the State of Rondonia. It was the Madeira-Mamore Railroad, but because of so many difficulties and so many deaths involved in the work, it was nicknamed "Devil's Railroad". However, before this venture, completed in 1912, produced results, the rubber produced in Southeast Asia, where today Laos, Malaysia and Vietnam are, generated by rubber tree seedlings that had been transplanted years before from the Amazon to there by English merchants, began to compete in the international market, in a destructive way. Even today, rubber is one of the riches generating foreign exchange for Vietnam and neighboring countries. After this phase, in the early 1930s, Henry Ford attempted to revive the wealth period of northern Brazil by financing the construction of an artificial city, Fordland, on the banks of the Tapajos River, near Belem and Santarem, but investment did not reverse the downfall 20 years earlier and the work became a ghost town.

With the loss of exclusivity in the supply of rubber, the Amazon kept stagnant deforestation, although many families in the Northeast continued to migrate to the region. Getting out of the dry areas and going to the Amazon, of superabundant water, it was almost like moving to paradise. As this migration cooled, in the early 1960s, the population of Manaus was less than 100,000.

It happened that the same government that started the construction of Brasilia to be the new capital of Brazil, headed by Lieutenant Colonel Juscelino Kubitschek, also approved the Law 3,173, of June 6, 1957, creating the Manaus Free Zone, which happened to be regulated and implemented by decree-law in 1967, already in the military regime inaugurated in 1964. It is an industrial area in which are exempt from taxes the companies that are installed in it.

With these two new drivers of development, the construction of Brasilia and the installation of the Manaus Free Zone, the acceleration of deforestation, human occupation and population growth increased sharply. At the end of the military regime, in 1985, the population of Manaus was over one million people, having been thus multiplied by ten, and today, on the eve of the 2020 census, is 2.13 million. It is the population that the city of Sao Paulo, largest city of South America, had in the year of 1950.

With the new Brazilian economic crisis started in the second half of 2013, successive governments have been celebrating a reduction in the acceleration of deforestation. We cannot foresee the time when the fall in rhythm will be celebrated, because the political effort in this sense is little or no. Taking up economic growth, almost certainly the previous level of tree clearing and transformation of large areas into pasture returns.

It should be noted that not only those two factors, the Free Trade Zone and Brasilia, have intensified the attack on the rainforest. The most damaging event came with a device incorporated into the 1988 Constitution. There was a consolidation of the understanding that property must have a social purpose, which is fair. The problem is that it was determined that land without crop husbandry would be considered "unproductive land", and such a land could be expropriated for agrarian reform.

Farmers who owned large tracts of virgin forest rushed to cut down their trees and fill their lands with grass, allocating one cow to every ten square miles. No one could say now that these properties contained "unproductive land".

Before this crop of grassland invaded the Amazon, it devastated the Atlantic Forest, since in this area the human occupation is older and denser. In the 20 years following the promulgation of the new Constitution, coastal states have lost practically all of their forest areas that have not been listed. As trees not only have the role of photosynthesis, re-purification of the air we breathe, but also of protecting the sources of drinking water, the phenomenon of dry rivers has spread in Brazil, something that was characteristic only of the Northeast Region. In the East, the South and the Midwest, the country began to see permanent rivers transform into temporary rivers. Laws were approved requiring the maintenance of the riparian forests, which are the fillets of afforestation along the waterways, mainly near the springs. This, however, almost nothing solves, because the humidity must be maintained in the soil in general, so that there is protection of the water tables.

Another problem to interfere with the health of the forest, though to a lesser extent, was a series of rumors circulating on the Internet since the end of the 20th century, according to which there was a plot of powerful countries plotting to withdraw from Brazil, as well as Peru and Colombia, the jurisdiction over the Amazon, transforming it into an area of international protection. Packed in this subterranean conversation, many politicians began to preach the intensification of human occupation in the region, to function as a kind of barricade.

The only way to reverse that error of the 1988 constituents and other destructive impulses will be to establish fiscal incentives for landowners who practice reforestation to a large extent of their properties, and to change the concept of "unproductive land" to include consensus of which land that sustains forest is, yes, productive.

It is known today that part of the Amazon rainforest is not exactly natural. Centuries before the arrival of Europeans, indigenous people have replanted trees in certain areas. This is an important precedent. Farmers now have a chance to reforest much larger farmland, rebuilding the forest to the extent that it is wholesome for our survival. Surely this restoration will not take place in five or ten years, but much longer. However, if we stop the clearing of forests and begin the tree recovery of the now deceptively productive lands, we will be signaling to the world that our part in the work of the planet's salvation is under way.

**Carbon**. One of the results of the Kyoto Protocol was the creation of the Carbon Credit market. There is an exchange field, which is regulated by the Clean Development Mechanism (CDM), according to which countries with high carbon dioxide emissions buy rights, which are the "surplus" quotas of countries with less developed industrial park and therefore produce less pollutants. This was a proven way of compensating the less industrialized countries for the effort to keep emitting little amount of greenhouse gases.

With a value change similar to that of a stock exchange on a daily basis, the Carbon Credit market defined as unit a ton of $CO_2$ equivalent, $tCO_2e$, which is the total emitted in greenhouse gases multiplied by its global warming potential. It is the responsibility of the Executive Board of the CDM to award to the bidders the Certified Emission Reduction, in which the amount of $tCO_2e$ is reduced or removed from the environment.

Not only between countries there are exchanges, but also between companies. Large polluters buy excess credits from those that pollute little and, therefore, can accumulate credit. This is the so-called "cap and trade" mechanism.

Some institutions around the world are responsible for organizing these transactions in the Carbon Credit market. In the United States the main ones are the CCX (Chicago Climate Exchange), the RGGI (Regional Greenhouse Gas Initiative) and the WCI (Western Climate Initiative).

In Europe, the system used is cap and trade, which involves 31 countries. Participants are allowed to purchase carbon credits from countries outside the continent, but in limited quantities.

In Brazil, carbon credit transactions are made through BM & FBovespa auctions, through requests made by public or private entities.

The creation of the Carbon Credit market, as it turns out, does not aim to reduce the level of pollution, but to establish a system of trade that reduces the growth of pollution. Without the mechanism, all countries would tend to become major emitters of greenhouse gases in the future.

As a system has already been put in place to prevent the rush of pollution, it is up to society to pursue sustainable development and reduce environmental damage wherever possible. Following the recommendations of the CSIC, seen above, is a path that we need to take if we do not already do it.

**Petroleum**. The Industrial Revolution, as we know, was moved to firewood and coal. In 1830 George Stephenson installed the world's first commercial railroad between Liverpool and Manchester, traversed by steam locomotives, which in Latin America were nicknamed "Smoke Marias", because of their wood-fired boilers. A few years earlier, Robert Fulton tried his steamboat on the Seine in 1803, but finding no support in France, he created the first regular ferry line in 1807, sailing across the Hudson River between Albany and New York, in the United States. This machine, the pyroscaphe, first designed by Roger Bacon in the thirteenth century, and unsuccessfully mounted by some inventors in the following centuries, only happened to function regularly with the investment of Fulton, and followed the principle that later Stephenson used in the trains, this is the steam-generating boiler, a practical use for the toy called aeolipile, invented by Hero of Alexandria in antiquity, and consisted of a metallic vessel with water, in the form of a rotating flask, which when heated, released in opposite directions two flows of steam that made it spin around an axis, like a weathervane. Fulton's boat won the world under the nickname "steam", from steamboat. However, firewood, charcoal, and also mineral coal did not subsist as industry drivers, for at the beginning of the twentieth century the large-scale use of petroleum derivatives began, and this became the energy base of progress since then.

While producing less smoke, but much more atmospheric pollution, the use of oil served to awaken us to the human capacity for destruction of nature.

The product was nothing new. Around the year 2000 BC, a kind of bitumen was used in the Babylon to pave the streets and in the Persian Empire the rich used oil in their lamps instead of olive oil.

In the seventh century, the Japanese referred to oil with an expression equivalent to burning water, indicating that they used it in lighting, as the Chinese did too. As early as the twentieth century, Persian and Arab researchers, including those in the Iberian Peninsula, obtained a kind of kerosene from crude oil for lighting purposes. When the Spaniards arrived in Venezuela at the end of the fifteenth century, they saw that the natives used oil for medicinal purposes and also paved their roads with bitumen.

In 1850 Scottish chemist James Young patented a method of extracting oil that resulted in fine oil, suitable for use as lamp oil, which became a kind of solid paraffin, and another type of thicker oil, used as a lubricant of machinery. As early as 1850, Canadian geologist Abraham Pineo Gerner created a method of refining oil that allowed him to obtain a fine fuel that he called kerosene. In 1854 he installed the North American Kerosene Gas Light Company in Long Island, USA, which was responsible for street lighting. The oil industry has begun to spread. Before that time, the practice of using whale oil in lighting increased. So, not everything is a mistake in the new era, for it would have happened without coal and oil, the extinction of whales in the oceans.

But it was the use of gasoline and diesel in car engines in the early twentieth century that led the world to embrace all at once the "oil age". Also in maritime transport it was soon found that the use of petroleum, instead of coal, allowed to develop higher speeds.

In 1909, following the discovery of vast oil reserves in what is now Iran, it was created the Anglo-Persian Oil Company, which in 1954 became the British Petroleum Company.

In 1927 it was discovered in Kirkuk, Iraq, which was then the largest oil well in the world.

In Saudi Arabia oil exploration began with the discovery of Dammam No. 7 well in 1938. With several successive discoveries of new fields, the country came to be seen as the world's largest source of the product, culminating with the discovery in 1948 of the Ghawar Field, the largest in the world today.

In 1960 the First Arab Oil Congress was held to create a price control mechanism, given the successive price reductions decided by some countries in isolation. By the agreement signed in that Congress, no country, from that moment, would make a decision to lower its prices without consulting the others. In September, a conference of participants from Iraq, Iran, Kuwait, Saudi Arabia and Venezuela opened OPEC, the Organization of Petroleum Exporting Countries.

There was not much talk about this entity until in 1973, with the realization that oil has limited reserves and in a few years will be exhausted, it happened the "oil crisis", when OPEC decided to raise prices, to ensure billing that will give a comfortable future to its members. This pressure lasted until 1979, when, realizing that alternative energies began to be developed and used, as it was the case with Brazil's ethanol, OPEC agreed to reduce the value of the oil barrel a little. Since then, prices have been wavering, with a downward trend in the 21$^{st}$ century, as the world approaches the time of the depletion of reserves and, in an accelerated fashion, implements the use of other energy modalities, such as biofuel, hydrogen, solar energy and the electrical network.

In any case, since 1973, much of the world's wealth has been transferred to oil well owners in the Middle East, but in most cases the populations of the region will not become direct beneficiaries of this new reality, since they live in incipiently democratic or even undemocratic regimes. It is a fact that some cities, since the end of the twentieth century, have experienced an outbreak of development, but they are like small oases in a great desert.

The end of the "oil age" will not only breathe the health of the environment but will also give America, Europe and the Far East the ability to supply their energy needs without depending on Arab and Iranian tycoons.

## Chapter 3 – Education and attitude

**Science**. Primary school teachers know that children absorb the principles of sustainable development and general environmental care much more easily than adults. Obviously, the ease of learning simple facts at an early age is always greater than in old age, but in the case of environmentalism this brings very prospective perspectives to the world. Faced with this, what is necessary is not to lower the guard.

Children will not discover on their own that the world is in great danger from the pressures exerted by adults on it. They see the horizon, the clouds and the stars, without being able to imagine that the actions of beings as tiny as we humans have enough destructive power to interfere with the life course of plants and animals as species. They know that a man can destroy the life of his neighbor, but they do not know by mere observation that the neighbor of a South American can be an inhabitant of Russia, India or Israel. The Butterfly Effect does not make sense to someone who has not yet been instructed on the issue, and one cannot convey this type of idea to anyone who has not had a minimum of notion of Physics. (According to the Butterfly Effect, when one of these beautiful insects flies in Chicago, United States, it may be causing a torrential storm in Sydney in the next few minutes. This has nothing to do with the notion of "parallel histories", an idea explored in two fiction films released under the title "Butterfly Effect".)

Do not think that Physics is a tangle of algebraic formulas. The most sophisticated concepts of this science could and should be taught in the primary cycle of the school, formed by the first two basic triennials, of children from six to 11 years old, abstracting from these concepts the mathematical arsenal that begins to be incorporated in the eighth grade, already within the junior high school, the third triennium of the regular school. The reader should remember the temperature conversion formulas even if he cannot reproduce them at this time.

Just as we introduced basic notions of biology to the "planting" of seeds in soggy cotton, with no need for accounts, except perhaps the measure of the time elapsed between the stages of germination, so we can teach topics in Physics and Chemistry. Arithmetic, in depth and legitimate, presents itself in the problems of Geometry, in lengths, areas and volumes, without any fright, and without headaches. But in Physics, concepts are worth. Accounts and equations enter the eighth grade, the ninth grade, and the high school grades, and then, if they are in lack, if the teacher insists on presenting only concepts without quantification, one is faced with a dishonest instructor. For the phase of purely qualitative concepts remained behind, in the elementary course.

One should not interpret this initial stage of introduction of science without calculations as being of little sophistication. Nor should we understand this sophistication as difficult, for it is not. Natural science is much more accessible to children and adolescents than the humanistic knowledge represented in Art, Philosophy and Literature, which are also introduced at the right time.

With germination experiments in the biological sciences and many others that can be done in physical sciences, such as those involving leverage, buoyancy, communicating vessels, air pressure, and so forth, the child soon becomes master of the notion of cause and effect. This understanding is essential for the person to accept, for example, the report that three men landed on the surface of the Moon in 1969. To fully understand this feat the young man must have learned about speed, acceleration, vectors, air resistance, orbits planetary and gravitation, which will only occur in High School, but already in the primary course he can absorb the information if he experienced the working of science, in a school that fulfills its role adequately.

A school or system of education that is minimally responsible does not deprive its children of the teaching of science in the above-mentioned ways, taking advantage of the age when the human brain is the "sponge", which easily absorbs the knowledge presented, according to Maria Montessori. Over the years, this sponge becomes more and more swollen, without so much openness through which new information can enter, according to recent Psychology studies, to which approximately half of the information, or training, in a person's life reaches him to the seven years, with another fourth being absorbed up to 14 years old.

All these consciences point to the categorical imperative of providing the children with a system of education with no space for amateurs or Romanticisms that will compromise the development of the contents that justify the existence of the school institution, that instrument created by Pythagoras to prepare in Mathematics and Philosophy of the young people who had recently left the Paideia, the kindergarten of literacy of antiquity, without them having to wait for the adult years to enter the army or, for some lucky ones among them, in the professional courses of the time, as for example that of tax collectors.

If most of the world's educational systems work properly by providing reasonable education to their children, then most young people will be prepared to close ranks in favor of a planet that cultivates sustainable development.

**Humanities**. The illusion that absorbing humanistic content in elementary school is easier than learning accounts and natural sciences has spread throughout the world. The reason for this is the form of evaluation in humanities, which, with exceptions, is more condescending than that applied in the scientific area.

Many high school sophomores are able to develop complicated computer programs, especially in the field of gaming. Finding a young man of the same age and training who, in his own words, speaks about a phase of history, for example, the first phase of the French Revolution, this is practically a miracle. Certainly, following a "PowerPoint" and commenting on the "slides" that are going on is a task that any teenager can fulfill, and that is not what this is all about.

Although many continue in the illusion, the assimilation of humanistic subjects in the days of the first letters is much more costly than the scientific learning. The Japanese government, which in 1869 decided to universalize primary education, which was successfully done, made the right decision to emphasize science, and, at the suggestion of a selfless group of intellectuals, the *boujins* (bystanders), according to Peter Drucker, also value reading, systematically. Those intellectuals, offering support to the emperor in his educational measure, requested of him support to travel by all the villages of the country in work of conscientization of directors and teachers on the importance of to form in the children the habit of the reading. The success was virtually complete, for Mutsuhito, the emperor who was also a great poet, secured the structural conditions for that cultural mission.

To solve problems of Arithmetic or Geometry and to answer questions of natural sciences is necessary to know how to read. To answer questions of the humanities, it is necessary to know how to read as well or better than for those other subjects. The habit of reading is, therefore, a foundation for schooling to work to the satisfaction. Teaching any subject in High School to students who are lazy to read, simply because they have not acquired the habit of reading in previous grades, is very exhausting. In contrast, teaching for student readers is a gift from the heavens that teachers receive.

If the students have become good readers, then they will be better able to learn topics of Geography, History, Grammar, Music, and, at high school, also Philosophy, Politics and Microeconomics.

Along with mental development, physical development must also be an indispensable object in school, which is done through gymnastics, including sports activities, but this field is linked to science as a biological area, not to the humanities.

The reader student will not burn steps, so one should not expect him to understand passages in human history to the depths of a learned adult. But he will assimilate facts with ease, which will allow him, in the measure of his chronological and intellectual maturity, to connect concepts and become lords of substantial knowledge.

If the child recalls that the year Christopher Columbus arrived in the New World was 1492, and this is consolidated in her head, a fool is the teacher who despises this conquest, armed with the destructive mystique of the second half of the twentieth century that preached condemnation to memorization. Now, whoever did not memorize essential facts while studying, he built his apprenticeship as an architect who mounts his house in the sand in an area of frequent vendors. This persecution of memorization came from a confusion the teachers made about a formulation of Maria Montessori. It has in fact dismantled the pattern of teaching that has existed since at least the Middle Ages until the nineteenth century, based on the practice of "memorizing for memorizing". The heuristic, the acquisition of the result by deduction, was completely neglected. But what she did not want was just this teaching that only accepts what is memorized, uncritically. She never overlooked memorization, which is essential for the construction of knowledge. And that kind of cogitation would not fit in the head of a doctor, as she was.

Until the first years of the twentieth century, if the child did not memorized the table, he would pick up either the teacher or his colleagues. It was "education through fear". This kind of practice has been abandoned almost everywhere in the world. A small proportion of children do not need to memorize the table to know it, and can arrive at the results by pure deduction. Another large part, most, only retains memorizing. Now, this must be done over the years, by practice. If the child accounts at school every day since the age of six, in three or four years the entire table should be in his head, even if he is too slow to learn. Thus, with repetition over repetition in daily exercises, it is easy to assimilate the contents.

How to assimilate then facts from the humanities, which do not have a basis of daily repetition? The answer is that they should be passed on whenever possible. If the teacher asks questions about Physical Geography in the class, these questions repeat themselves, and the right answers as well. If the question is, for example, what is the capital of China, the first student can make a mistake, but the second can do it right. With the teacher emphasizing the right answer, soon the class will assimilate the result. Days later, he turns to the same theme. And so the learning is consolidated. When the vast majority has this answer firmly in mind, the subject can be left out, and the very slow ones will learn up front if that is necessary. Because the student does not need to hit 100% of the questions to be considered fit, neither should the teacher wait until 100% of the class learns a topic to move on.

Since the 1980s, Secondary School has incorporated a chapter on Ecology in the Biology curriculum. Also at the elementary level, as early as the first triennium, basic notions of this theme must be introduced. Regardless of whether or not we believe in global warming, today there is no reasonably well-informed individual who denies the importance of knowledge about sustainability issues. Only fools like to live surrounded by polluted rivers, breathing contaminated air and stepping on dirt in the streets.

With more humanized and at the same time efficient methods, school can play its role of teaching, bringing basic learning to all children. And then they will be able to take care of nature, to treat wisely their common home, which is their environment.

**Attitude**. After being alerted to the fragility of life on Earth, given the risks to nature itself and to the reckless actions of the human species, children begin to seek ways to contribute to the security of the planet, for the implementation of sustainable development at all levels. How to pollute less or avoid pollution? How can we help family and colleagues address the issue of solid waste recycling in the most environmentally friendly way possible? How to avoid discarding used kitchen oil in the environment? How to convince parents to buy cars that use clean energy? How to save water? How to prevent rivers from being damaged by sewage disposal in them? How to avoid the advance of global warming? All these and other questions are questions children begin to ask themselves, their colleagues and adults, after they become aware of the environmental problem.

In the matter of recycling, children's willingness to separate dry garbage from organic waste is well known and even to require adults to have a sustainable attitude towards the problem.

Schools make a serious mistake because when they mix organic canteen waste with recyclable waste like paper and plastic in front of children. Children certainly look at these things and think, "How stupid adults are!"

In order not to reverse this positive view of children, we adults must meet their expectations, respecting the rules of recycling and acting in accordance with these dictates.

The municipal public power should exercise severe vigilance on the issue of solid waste separation. Forwarded to landfills should be only organic garbage completely free of glass, plastic or metal parts, or environmentally harmful chemical materials, and it should already arrive crushed to the destination, so to integrate to the ground. Citizens who deliver organic garbage to the collection service without the recyclable separations should be duly fined.

In schools, students should be involved in the recyclable collection and, whenever possible, managers and teachers should make them realize that this is a source of income. In France there are "school cooperatives", which use recycling as a means of earning income, with the help of students. Other countries may institute equivalent systems. Paper, which still produces the highest volume of solid waste, is low priced as recyclable material, but aluminum, plastic and other products are of higher value. In any case, the monetary value does not matter much, when what matters most is the attitude of contributing to the health of the environment.

From an early age, the infantile custom of kneading the paper like a ball, then throwing it in the wastebasket, must be reoriented. The paper used, which goes to the trash, should be kept stretched, without folds, to facilitate its storage and separation. If this learning takes place, the treatment of other types of solid waste will also be better organized.

## Chapter 4 - Risks

**Asteroids**. The greatest risk in terms of danger, but of very low probability value, is that of being hit by a large unruly star, a rock the size of the Moon, for example.

Astronomers know from observation of space that by the year 2170, for at least a century and a half at least, the chance of a massive bolt colliding with the Earth is practically zero. For the following centuries there is no prediction, but it is certain that one day it will come a great star to cause us a definitive damage. So one of the missions of scientists in the future will be to design an anti-missile system not to intercept projectiles from enemy armies, but to shatter giant meteors before they destroy us.

Craters of the Moon, craters of Mars and gulfs in the Earth's oceans are, in many cases, the result of clashes of large asteroids. In even more remote times, the moons themselves on the various planets in which they orbited arose from these shocks. In the Solar System, the interval between such a collision and the next one can be of millennia on average, but nothing prevents that within two centuries it will not be the turn of our planet to be hit once more. So we have to invest in prevention if we are here.

Supernova. A star shines through its use of its nuclear energy. Many of them reach a stage where they are transformed into supernovae by violent explosion, which releases gamma, beta and X rays in colossal quantities in an equally large radius.

If we were close enough to the Solar System to be sufficiently large to become supernovae, this would be one of the greatest risks of extinction on earth because it would compromise our atmosphere. This phenomenon, however, has occurred many light-years away from our planet and the chance that a supernova damages Earth is very tiny, almost zero. Our star, the Sun, is small in size to explode as a supernova, and it is predicted for it a few million years of active existence.

**Supervolcanoes**. A supervolcano is a volcano that not only expels lava to reach a radius of a few kilometers, but, as it was the case of Krakatoa, in Indonesia, in 1883, causes destruction of entire islands and even countries. After the eruption, tsunamis can cause damage on the opposite shore of the ocean even tens of thousands of miles away. The appearance of its smoke is that of an atomic bomb.

Earthquakes, tsunamis and volcanoes are extensively studied, but to this day science has not reached the means of mapping its future activities.

If, by some misfortune, supervolcanoes erupt at various points on the globe at the same time, life on the planet will run the risk of disappearing. This, however, seems to be a remote possibility.

**Bacteria**. The sterilization of medical instruments before surgery, as recommended by Louis Pasteur and Joseph Lister, avoided major killings since the mid-nineteenth century. Humanity before that, however, was in the hands of the germs, as happened with the black plague epidemics that devastated Europe, since it was unintentionally scattered on the continent by Genghis Khan's troops.

Nowadays, the chance of a bacterium, or a virus, that exterminates human life is almost zero, but it exists. When the AIDS virus emerged, the surprise that came together is that it was a microbe with a double coating, which made it difficult for almost two decades to develop medicines that would fight against it. And the worst thing is that it attacked people's immune system, i. e., exactly achieved the protection the body has against invading viruses and unwanted bacteria.

So there is no way to ensure that no other harmful microorganism emerges by breaking down all the barriers we have already built against these inferior beings. Until now, what is known is that in any epidemic there are people who are resistant, who do not allow themselves to be contaminated, which also happened in the face of the AIDS virus.

However small, the risk of being exterminated by microorganisms exists.

**Waste**. The four threats listed above run away from our ability to manipulate so far, although the latter, that of microorganisms, is in some way under our control, given the knowledge we have already accumulated on the subject, which includes our role in combating these beings through antibiotics since the first half of the twentieth century. But the threat posed by the waste we throw into the environment is the fruit of our decisions. The plastic waste thrown in the dumps, in the woods and in the waters of the rivers and the oceans will not dissolve in the next centuries and already it has been causing damage to the life of other alive beings. Acids and other products discarded and dumped into rivers and soil by factories can also pose major problems in the long run, including pesticides. Chlorofluorocarbon (CFC) used in refrigerators and aerosols can deteriorate the ozone layer that protects the atmosphere against harmful radiation. Fortunately, awareness and positive actions have already led to a reversal in the use of this product. But what about nuclear waste, generated by atomic power plants, which will be stored dangerously for thousands of years? Among the forms of clean energy, it certainly does not appear to be the result of the fission power plants at their present stage. It is urgent to move to safer plants.

**Deforestation**. The effect of deforestation on the life of species is very serious. With the accelerated clearing of forests in Brazil between the 1990s and 2010, farmers began to lament the lack of bees, which work on pollination of certain crops. Bees, in fact, fade away as humans tear down their natural abodes, which are the trees. But many other wild species, of larger animals, disappeared, some even before being cataloged. In recent times, jaguars have invaded urban areas, perhaps seeing more trees in backyards than in their ancient forests. Without forests, as has been said above, the sources of drinking water do not sustain themselves, and this has increased the periods of drought. And carbon dioxide emissions will no longer be absorbed by not finding trees.

**War**. The UN was created in 1945, after the defeat of Nazism, as an entity designed to promote peace and prevent a third world war. However, we know that it works on the basis of negotiation, with no authority to prevent the outbreak of this conflict if there is a sufficiently strong motive for its occurrence. The risk of a world war still exists and can be fatal to the existence of mankind and other species, since the use of nuclear weapons and chemical weapons would hardly be excluded from the process. Countries under dictatorships, theocracies or absolutist regimes continue to produce regional conflicts and are the focus that can draw the great powers to the disastrous event of global war. Western Europe and the Americas seem to be free of the phenomenon, but the UN has no power to wipe out from the face of the earth those backward and unhealthy forms of government that are still sustained in Asia, the Middle East, and Africa.

**Heating**. As already discussed above, global warming, with almost 100% certainty, has been occurring by the human hand. We do not have a prognosis today of what could happen to the Earth soon after the disappearance of all ice from the polar ice caps. What will the animals do on the ice? What will happen to them? If the oceans do not have much to increase in volume, the heat waves provoke movements of the seas in a way that was not known before. Great hangovers are destroying coastal buildings in a way we have never seen. Hurricanes have increased their frequency and destructive power. The range of temperatures has grown, with much more intense colds and hot flashes that have killed people and animals. Those who have political or economic power have a great responsibility in the matter, but also the simple consumer, who demand and buy the products that the industry strives to offer us, play a very important role in reversing these facts, if at all there is still the possibility.

**Overpopulation**. The diversity of living beings obeys natural laws that determine what is called ecological balance, with some species being part of the food chain of others. The absence of sufficient predators can cause serious problems to nature, and this may be due to natural disasters or human interference. It is said that at a certain time in the Middle Ages cats were eliminated in Europe, because the myth that they were demonized and brought bad luck circulated there. The result within a few years was that the population of rats had spread in the cities in an unusual way, leading to outbreaks of leptospirosis and other diseases. Very prolonged periods of drought, in a non-standard situation, can cause the disappearance of certain species and change the eating habits of others.

In the human species, the development of intelligence and consciousness endowed individuals with resources to escape from natural selection, replacing it with artificial selection. Our predators, on the one hand, with the large carnivorous animals, and on the other with the tiny animals, the microorganisms, were dominated by the invention of weapons and techniques of domestication, for the bigger ones, and, in the case of microbes, ointments, fermentations, vaccines and, finally, antibiotics, in an era started with the publication of the Scottish doctor Alexander Fleming, in 1929, on the discovery of penicillin.

While dominating the upper and lower predators, the human species discovered that it was the mistress of the world. Even before the firearms and the great pharmacological discoveries of modern times, other simpler mechanisms already allowed mankind to protect itself in a way that other animal species never succeeded. The beginning of the use of clothing, followed by the creation of religion, which strengthened tribal ties, and later, city, government, education, legislation, and science, all gave mankind a great power over nature. Thus, the human species might grow inordinately. The most populous countries, such as China and India, pay the price of having invented cities before others. The older the cities of the country, the greater its population, and there is no relation to the presence of "good governments", as some romantic philosophers have irresponsibly written.

Frequent wars, which were a tragic mechanism of restraining the population growth, have been diverted to less civilized areas of the Earth and may be extinguished in a few decades.

In the 1960s the contraceptive pill was developed, and this seemed to provide the solution to the problem of overpopulation, but it helped the countries of educated populations, who somehow already exercised birth control by natural methods, leaving countries poor and little educated almost in the same condition as before.

There is also, to counterbalance the benefit that the pill brought, the increase in longevity, something always desirable if the supply of natural resources were absolutely elastic or the high number of applicants did not threaten the balance. In 1789 the average living in France, the most advanced country in the world at that time, before England perfected French inventions and created the Industrial Revolution, was 29 years. In 1900 the average life expectancy in the world was 31 years, going to 72 years at the beginning of 2018. Since longevity more than doubled in just over a century, each individual occupies the place that was occupied by two, of the world population.

From the year 1 AD to the year 1,000, i. e., in the first millennium of our era, the estimated world population grew from 200 million to 300 million, meaning a 50% increase. In the second millennium, from 1,000 to 2,000, the population jumped to more than 6,000 million (6 billion), in an increase of 1,900%.

Since the birth of Homo sapiens in Morocco, 250,000 years ago, only in the year 1825, approximately, the world population reached its first billion members. Those who think that population growth is no problem should meditate on the fact that another billion people have been added to the world only in the first 11 years of the 21st century. Another new billion is added in the year 2018, making a total of 8,000,000,000 of similar to us.

Whenever we see a species spreading in an overwhelming way, overcoming predators, we understand that we are facing a plague. If there were on Earth an animal species superior to us in intelligence and consciousness, I would clearly realize that we are today the great plague of the planet. Among us, differently, there is a portion that sees overpopulation as a huge danger to life on Earth and there is another great part ridiculing this kind of vision, preaching in four winds that the human population can grow without limits, without causing great problems.

**Interviews**. In interviews given to newspapers and magazines, Hawking listed, at different times, five risks to life. The first was that of microorganisms, in the form of bacteria or viruses that can be raised in the laboratory and, by a disaster, get out of control. The second, almost certainly the least likely, is that of Aliens. Some intelligent species from another planet can have their resources depleted and depart around the universe seeking new means of subsistence, finally reaching the Earth. His arrival may be, for us humans, far more disastrous than the arrival of Columbus for the peoples of the Americas. The third risk is far above despicable and deals with Artificial Intelligence. As in the case of laboratory microorganisms, the development of computing technology can reach a point where we are left inferior and dependent on machines, which, unlike Hall, the "2001 Space Odyssey" computer (Arthur C. Clarke, filmed by Stanley Kubrick in 1968), cannot be turned off by us. Although one reading of Kurt Gödel's Incompleteness Theorem is that the intelligence of machines will not surpass human intelligence, there is no absolute assurance about it. The fourth major risk is that of Nuclear War. This is perhaps the most frightening and, at the same time, the one that demands more attention on the part of rulers and scientists. Since the fall of the Berlin Wall in November 1989 and the consequent end of the Cold War, the world should have invested heavily in disarmament policies, but this is still an ongoing project. Finally, the fifth risk is Global Warming.

To indicate the state of the world's risk of destruction by atomic conflicts and anthropogenic warming, Hawking and other scientists readjust the *Doomsday Clock* in London, in 2007, to the time 5 minutes to midnight, meaning midnight the total destruction of life. This timetable incorporates the risk embedded in the use of fossil fuels in vehicles, industry, deforestation and intensive livestock farming. Since January 2017, the pointer is indicating 2 minutes to midnight. The Clock was established in 1947, two years after the explosion of the two atomic bombs over Japan.

## Chapter 5 - Krypton and the imagination

**Superpower**. In 1932, Irene Joliot-Curie and her husband Frédéric Joliot identified the neutron, within the structure of the atom, demonstrating the possibility of artificial alteration of the nucleus. That same year, Wolfgang Pauli and Enrico Fermi, among others, studied and published works that would deepen this idea.

From this knowledge circulating in the press, it happened the inspiration in 1933 for the Superman saga. A scientist from a distant planet, called Krypton, found in his calculations that the star where he lived would suffer a violent explosion, nothing left of it but shards roaming the space. This scientist, Jor-El, was the father of a child, an only child, called Kal-El. Unable to embark adults on space travel, he built a small spacecraft, on which, on the eve of the great catastrophe, he and his wife would send their child through the skies of Krypton. If he was very lucky, the boy would land on Earth, a planet very similar to that, although with a much smaller force of gravity.

Descending on Earth, and falling into the backyard of a couple of childless farmers, the boy is raised by the name of Clark Kent. As he grows up, he discovers that he possesses special qualities in comparison to similar Earthlings, such as abnormal force, steel-consistent body, X-ray vision, and by the difference in gravity between his planet and ours, the power to fly. Migrating to the big city he devotes himself to journalism, working on the Daily Planet, and decides to create an alternative personality, Superman, to help the authorities do justice. Not even Lois Lane, his fellow essayist and quasi-girlfriend, who is often seconded to cover Superman's exploits, realizes that he and the shy Clark Kent are the same person. Lex Luthor, a jealous Clark schoolmate, later discovered that certain mysterious meteorites, fallen to Earth as a result of the Krypton explosion, had, in green mode, the power to nullify Superman's advantages over humans. Even more serious, the red mode of kryptonite could kill that alien.

Obviously, Jerry Siegel and Joseph Shuster, the authors of the comic-book saga, knew that they could not invent an Achilles without the problem of heel vulnerability. But over the years and decades, Superman has always been able to escape kryptonite attacks.

**Stories**. Few scientists deny the influence they received in their teenage years, from science fiction readings, in books such as those of Mary Shelley, Jules Verne and HG Wells, from the late 19th to early twentieth century and in comics and middle from the twentieth century onwards. In the 21st century, the genre has retreated, because the impression that youth has is that reality has overcome fiction in terms of technological advances, and there has been a drop in the level of learning in most countries. Perhaps the imagination of the writers is that it is very much attached to the present reality, or perhaps it is not possible to distinguish, even in the midst of the profusion of available works, which is representing a minimally palpable future, without merely playful fantasies. The TV series *Star Trek*, for example, the creation of Gene Roddenberry, returned in the late twentieth century in 1987 as *Star Trek: The New Generation*, and it was until May 1994, when he presented the last episode, but it, however successful, did not arouse the enthusiasm of the previous one. In this new generation, space mission occurs in the XXIV century, a century after the events of the original series, begun in 1966. In both cases, the objective of the trip is to explore the universe, finding new worlds, especially those inhabited by beings similar to us, and also studying other forms of life.

The new series was released on DVD from 2002 and its stories generated four films. In TV, the two phases totaled a total of 30 seasons.

One of the differences between the two phases is that in the new Klingon people, previously inimical to humans, began to form an alliance with the Terrans. The Romulans also appear in the new, but without changing in the animosity that they feed toward members of the mission.

Imbued with the new winds that circulated around the Earth in the late twentieth century, some episodes of the new series show the ship's crew's concern to seek ways to save the human species from destruction.

Despite bringing this lugubrious theme to the possibility of the end of our species in the coming centuries, Star Trek was a breath of hope for society. Women had positions of power, such as Commander Katherine Janeway, played by actress Kate Kulgrew, and a black woman, Michelle Nichols, played Lieutenant Uhura on an equal footing with the other military members of the ship. Struggling for the smooth running of the Federation of Planets, the own ship's crew was composed of members of various terrestrial ethnicities, including also an extraterrestrial, Dr. Spock. In the future, from the standpoint of the series, there will be no racial discrimination or war between humans, no money notes will be used and no distinction will be made between being commanded by woman or man.

Some of the advanced processes and products shown in the saga have already come true. Among them are the tablet; the touch screen; the intercom, which took shape in the cell phone; the headset; Dr. McCoy's examination machine, which "saw" the patient from the inside, and which became the CT scanner; and the doors that opened alone, in front of the approach of a person, and which are now used worldwide in shopping malls and other establishments.

**Sunshine**. In 2057 scientists find that the nuclear reaction of the Sun is evanescing, with the risk of our star going out much sooner than predicted and extinguishing life on Earth. A space mission is sent to, while reaching the vicinity of the star, pour into its gravitational field a huge nuclear bomb, which must have the power to reanimate its atomic activity. This is the axis for *Sunshine*'s narrative, 2007 film, directed by Danny Boyle, with screenplay by Alex Garland.

All the information we have predicted for millions of years ahead of our time this event, which is inevitable. But in fiction we can imagine any fact, being one of the most common to translate the time of the possible occurrence of natural phenomena. And the metaphor that can be grasped from this story is that scientists and technicians are willing to make sacrifices, voluntary or otherwise, in favor of humanity.

We have clear that, among the existing professional categories, there are groups that work as scouts, seeking guarantees to improve the lives of the populations of their respective countries and also to save them from external threats. They are made up of rulers, military and diplomats. The remaining economic agents form civil society. But few realize how scientists transcend this role, always striving to ensure improvement for all humanity, not for a country, and, on the most tense, trying to save humanity, whenever any threat is detected or glimpsed.

We cannot forget that Marie Curie, discoverer of the element radium, used her discovery during World War I working as a nurse and applying radiotherapy to the wounded of the battlefields, always accompanied by the eldest daughter, Irene. Without looking at the perverse side of radiation, he contracted cancer of the arm and died as a result. Other pioneers, also mentioned above, died of cancer, most likely initiated by radioactivity: Irene Joliot-Curie, Wolfgang Pauli and Enrico Fermi had this end.

**Beach**. In 1959 Stanley Kramer produced and directed the film *On the Beach*, based on the 1957 Neil Shute novel. With Gregory Peck, Ava Gardner, Fred Astaire and Anthony Perkins, the film is a alert against the Cold War and a severe criticism of that tension between the powers.

The fragile balance of the Cold War, aimed at avoiding World War III, breaks down at a given moment, and the great powers return to the battlefield, now with pulverized shots of nuclear artifacts. The Northern Hemisphere is all compromised. Officers from the United States Navy are close to Japan and are ordered to head south. They try to emerge in the Philippines, but there the air does not look friendly either. There is Australia, where they drop anchor. There, the cloud had not yet arrived.

An insistent telegraph signal is detected coming from California. Maybe someone's alive over there. In the same atomic submarine they landed in Australia, they go to San Francisco and San Diego to check what's going on. There is no one alive. They discover the cause of the signal emission, which is not human. They return to Australia. But the quiet is short.

**Happening**. In the 2008 film *The Happening*, director M. Night Shyamalan presents a story in which humans are attacked by a toxin that creates suicidal impulses in them. With Mark Wahlberg and Zooey Deschanel, the film addresses the issue of the possibility of destruction of mankind through microorganisms.

What is discovered, after many mishaps, is that the toxin is a response of the vegetation of the Earth to the destructive actions promoted by the human species, which has become a type of plague in front of other living beings.

**Tomorrow**. *The Day After Tomorrow*, 2004, directed by Roland Emmerich, is one of the most catastrophic films in the cinema history, not so much because of the scenes it shows, but because it is all very plausible, at least for those who accept the scientific conclusions about global warming.

With Dennis Quaid, Jake Gyllenhaall, Ian Holm and Emmy Rossum, the story begins with researchers in Antarctica, verifying, in practice, the effects of global warming. Jack Hall (Dennis Quaid), a climatologist, collects ice samples when a large block breaks off, nearly killing him. When he presents his findings at a conference in New Delhi a few days later, he faces, as might be expected, strong reactions amid enthusiastic support. From the model he developed, a new glaciation can occur on Earth in a short time, as a consequence of the climatic changes that humanity has been observing.

From one moment to the next, great tsunamis, hail, very violent hurricanes and terrible snowstorms hit many regions of the planet.

Almost at the end of the movie, astronauts observe the ice covering the Northern Hemisphere. Humanity was at great risk of disappearing, but it was not this time. Some who remain alive will have the task of repopulating the earth, and taking judgment.

In addition to the representative examples discussed above TV and cinema have hundreds of other works of fiction dealing with the end of the world or its proximity.

**Motivations**. It is clear that the two Great Wars and the possibility of a third, which would occur in ways similar to that portrayed in On the Beach, motivated the writing of countless works in this line.

After the US military dropped two nuclear bombs on Hiroshima and Nagasaki, on 6 and 9 August 1945, the world was faced with the prospect of destruction of humanity by atomic weapons if a new world war broke out as a consequence of the animosities of World War II, which, in turn, came as a result of the pending war left by the First World War.

In August 1939, physicists Albert Einstein and Leo Szilard wrote a letter to United States President Franklin Delano Roosevelt warning that the Nazis were investing in building an atomic bomb, which would allow them to win the war. The warning resulted in the Manhattan Project, building the atomic bomb in the United States. After the German Nazis had been defeated, the Japanese became more fierce combatants. As conventional weapons did not dissuade them, Harry S. Truman, then president of the United States, made the decision to bomb them with nuclear weapons.

In the early 1950s Einstein wrote some letters to Japanese friend Seiei Shinohara revealing his disappointment at what happened to Japan and his regret for having alerted Roosevelt. The concern was the German Nazis, who, in short, failed to complete their nuclear bomb project. Einstein wrote that if he knew in advance that his home country, Germany, would not get to build the bomb, he would never have signed the letter to Roosevelt. Einstein, as we all know, was a great admirer of Japan, which he took as an example in the area of education. And he was a convicted pacifist.

## Chapter 6 - Premonitions

**Dreams**. As we mentioned above, our ancestors said that the world was first destroyed by water and would eventually be destroyed by fire. Predictions about the end of the world, meaning the end of life on Earth, are common to almost every culture. And they are in literature, whether in clerical religious texts or in esoteric texts, without mentioning the speculative works of a secular nature.

Among the possible restrictions to the possibility of premonition is not the conflict with free will, for two reasons: First, many predictions are conditional, of the kind that ensures that something will occur in such a way if such a providence is not taken first; second, small events, of no historical importance, because they are routine or manipulative, and which are almost all occurrences in our life, are not the object of prophetic visions. If a seer "sees" a fact that will take place only a century later, it will not be a mundane event, but something grandiose, for good or for evil. And for each system or individual, everything that happens depends on internal injunctions or external forces. What depends only on external forces is beyond the reach of free will.

Anyone who has ever had an experience of "dejá vu", which is that feeling that the person has lived that moment before, not being able to specify when, this person was, almost certainly, experiencing the materialization of a premonition. Almost all of our dreams are forgotten during sleep itself, or even those remembered in the waking hours are erased from the mind in a short time. The dejá vu may have occurred in one of those dreams that the person cannot remember, no matter how he strains. But not all people are open to premonition. It is well known that the smoking habit distracts the person from this type of perception. Certain sexual practices may also prevent not only the possibility of sensory anticipation of future events, but also the willingness to accept the phenomenon.

Should we take the prophecies seriously? Not usually. Just as we should not buy any book of poems sold in any corner. For the citizen who respects Christian culture, even though he is agnostic, Paul of Tarsus says that we should not despise the prophecies *in totum*: "Teat all things, hold fast that what is good" (1 Thessalonians).

Regardless of whether the reader credits prophecy or not, and relying on skepticism instead of refractoriness, we turn to some visions of the future that some people have had, or others have reported they had, without spending time with what appears to be a false account.

**Rome**. Many prophecies are known about the destruction of the City of the Seven Hills, nickname of Rome. What few know is that the prediction about the end of the city arose in the year 753 BC, as soon as it was founded. It was said that Romulus, one of the twins who founded it (the other was Remus), was visited by 12 eagles, which revealed a secret. The first interpretation was that 12 years later the city would be destroyed, since each eagle should represent a year. As this did not happen, the prediction has been receiving varying interpretations, decade after decade, century after century.

**Jerusalem**. Almost seven centuries later, in the year 63 BC, Pompey conquered Israel, incorporating the region to Rome. Between 58 BC and 55 BC, Rome divided the area into the provinces of Judea, Samaria and Galilee, keeping Jerusalem as the capital. Perhaps by influence of the prophecy that foresaw the end of Rome, the Essenes, a branch of ascetics in Judaism, came to believe that Jerusalem would also come to an end, and when the war of Israel against Rome began in 66 AD, they saw in it the end of time for its capital. In fact, the city and the Second Temple of Solomon were destroyed by the Romans in AD 70. As we all know, the city did not disappear at all, and was restored in time.

Shortly before this tragedy, Jesus Christ, a religious preacher, cousin and follower of John the Baptist, taught, according to the biblical account, that the end was near, but no one but the Creator could hit the day. Looking at the city of Jerusalem from the mountain, he predicted, using a Greek saying, that there would not remain "stone upon stone". In this he may have sensed the impending destruction of the city. About the end of time, the mere mortals were given to recognize the proximity of the event by the signs. Earthquakes in various parts, many sicknesses, hunger raging on Earth, nation rising against nation, kingdom rising against kingdom, brother rebelling against brother, son rebelling against father, sons killing their own parents. They will be days of tribulation like never before since the creation of the world. False prophets will arise performing wonders to deceive simple people. If anyone says, "Here is the Christ", do not believe it. These things are not yet the end, according to Jesus, but only the signs.

After all these tribulations, Jesus of Nazareth said, and after the "good news", the word of the gospel, is taught all over the world, the sun will be darkened and there will be no light from the Moon. Stars will fall from heaven and the heavenly powers shall be shaken. Then the "Son of man", the Christ, with great power and glory will appear in the midst of the clouds, and he will send the angels and gather the elect from the ends of the Earth to the ends of the sky. Even with the signs, the anointed one, the Christ, would come by surprise, "like a thief in the night."

In the following decades, many believed that the end of time would come very briefly. Paul of Tarsus recommended that people not marry, generating new families, because the greatest concern would have to be preparation for the end, which would not be long in coming.

Once this could occur on any day, any year, is two millennia already, and the end has not yet come, but we should not reason as if these centuries we have gained were a denial of the prophecies. Whether by premonition or scientific evaluation, we know that the end of life on Earth will come, and just like prophecy, science also resents the ability to determine the date.

**Apocalypse**. The last book of the Bible, Apocalypse ("Revelation", in Greek), was written by John of Patmos. For the Catholic tradition, this John is the same one who was called "John the Presbyter", "John the Theologian", "John the Evangelist", and who was the youngest among the twelve apostles of Jesus. He was the son of Zebedee and brother of James the Greater, but, as in the book of Apocalypse he does not identify himself as one of the twelve, in modern times doubts of the early Christian centuries about his identity resurfaced. For some trends, he is another preacher. For Catholicism and several other Christian churches, he is the Apostle himself who was expelled from Ephesus by the Romans under the Emperor Domitian at the end of the first century when he evangelized in that city and exiled himself on the island of Patmos, in the Aegean Sea, where, in old age, wrote his final book. The letters he addresses to the seven Hellenic churches weigh heavily in favor of Catholic interpretation, since in this way he shows himself to be well known to these early churches, which would hardly occur to a novice. Another element little remembered is the question of the human factor. There were not many ministers involved in Christian doctrine in the first century, even less named John and at the same time with the talent for writing.

Although in the seventh century the Catholic Church turned into a heresy the denial of the Apostle John's writings to the text of the Apocalypse, early in the 21st century scholars of the Church themselves hypothesized that the work was written by someone from an alleged Johannine community, formed by disciples of the apostle, that could make happen by the own John.

According to Professor Scott Hahn, the United States theologian, there are four lines of interpretation for the book Apocalypse: preterists, which relate the symbols and facts of the work to figures of the first century; idealist, for whom the work exposes an allegory of the struggle between good and evil, to be embraced by Christians; historicist, according to which the book brings the divine plan of all human history, including the history of the Church; futurist, who identifies figures of the book with characters from history, seeing as beasts of the Apocalypse leaders such as Genghis Khan, Napoleon Bonaparte, Benito Mussolini, Adolf Hitler, Josef Stalin, Mao Zedong and others.

The book went through much controversy in the early centuries of the Catholic Church because of the refusal of many to consider it as a canonical text. The Orthodox Church has agreed to include it in the Bible, but to this day it forbids its reading in the liturgy. The fear was that millennialism gained momentum within Christian trends, with the risk of fanaticism and other deviations.

Four distinct parts make up the text: Letters to the Seven Churches, the Lamb and the Seven Seals, the Dragon, the New Jerusalem. In the first part, an old man with white hair and long robes, with seven stars in his hands and a sword in his mouth sends the message. In the next part, the Lamb is presented as one who can open the book of the Seven Seals. There arise the Four Horsemen of the Apocalypse, bringing plague, famine, war, and death. John presents in poetic language the vision of the signs that precede the end, according to the teaching of Jesus. From the opening of the Seven Seals it comes the touch of the Seven Trumpets, which announce more catastrophes. In the third part the Dragon and the Beasts of Apocalypse appear, one bearing the number 666. The seven bowls enter the scene, bringing other symbolisms. The Harlot, representing Great Babylon, symbolizing all vices, is protected by the Dragon and the Beasts. In the great battle of Armageddon, the Lamb comes on his white horse and Great Babylon is defeated, with the Beasts being cast on the lake of fire. The Dragon is arrested "for a thousand years and more". After this, he escapes and reunites the armies of Gog and Magog, beginning the final battle, when he is definitely defeated.

The New Jerusalem is represented by the whole Earth. There will be "new heavens and new lands", the book says.

Contrary to the negative connotation that the idea of Revelation came to have, as something that brings destruction to all, what John presents is the Christians' struggle to get rid of temptations, which do bring many misfortunes, plagues, wars and natural cataclysms. The message of John, after describing all these occurrences in allegorical language, is that the Lamb wins.

Unlike many other prophecies about the end of the world, John's Apocalypse is a message of hope.

Will we be literally dwelling on new planets under new heavens? Or will the New Jerusalem, which is our planet, undergo a well-deserved regeneration, giving human beings a healthy and happy life in the coming centuries? Three thousand years ago, almost every major event depended on circumstances greater than ourselves, from factors we could not control. In the third millennium of the Christian era, we are scouring the universe and we are interfering with the climate without even knowing how to make it work for us. Are we on our way? Yes, but we do not know if we'll have time.

**Millenarians**. The figure of the Antichrist appears for the first time in the epistles of the apostle John, not in the Apocalypse, which makes no reference to such an element. As he comes to work against the designs of Jesus Christ, according to the apostle, it was not difficult to identify him with the Dragon.

The millenarians almost always relate the end times, the Last Judgment, with the advent of the Antichrist, which would be the strongest signal to foretell the event.

St. Martin of Tours, a Hungarian saint, predicted that the end of time would occur in the year 400, or shortly before, stating that the Antichrist was already in the world in the fourth century.

It was not this time, but three other seers fixed in the year 500 that which did not occur in 400. They were St. Irenaeus, II century, Hippolytus of Rome and Sextus Julius Africanus, these of the third century. The latter ensured that if the end did not come in the year 500, it would come in the year 800.

The most credible date, however, was the entry of the year 1000. Although the papacy was in the hands of an enlightened man, St. Sylvester II, Father Gerbert, who had introduced into France the teaching of Indo-Arabic numerals, the uproar was immense, for many clergymen and many independent seers gambled on that year as the date of the end. The own Pope, just in case, prepared himself for the Last Judgment.

As the year 1000 ended without great upsets, the seers did not give up: they fixed the new date in the year 1033, which would be the sum of a thousand years and the age of Christ.

Following diverse arguments, other scholars continued to present new dates in the following decades and centuries. Thus the end was foreseen for 1186, 1260 and 1284. The next very convincing date was 1496, a year that would have completed a millennium and a half of the birth of Jesus, which had occurred, as it is understood, in the year 4 BC.

How about the year 1666? A great number of clairvoyants

worked with this number, which would be the millennium added to the 666 of the Beast of the Apocalypse. This was another wrong guess.

An English theologian who was also an astronomer, William Whiston, predicted the collision of a large comet with Earth to occur on October 16, 1736, bringing the end of the world.

Important ministers of the Quaker religion in the United States concluded that the second coming of Jesus Christ would occur in the year 1792. This was a year of effervescence in the French Revolution, but it was not the end. Then the same ministers readjusted the date for 1794.

William Miller, who founded the Adventist religion, predicted that Jesus would return in 1843 or 1844. Other Adventist ministers readjusted the date as the years went by without the end coming.

Later, Joseph Smith, founder of the Mormon religion, stated that the second coming of Jesus would be in the year 1891.

The next important leader to set a date was Charles Taze Russell, founder of Jehovah's Witness religion. For him, the end would occur in 1914. In that year World War I broke out, but it ended in 1918. New dates were being presented by Jehovah's Witnesses.

After some mystics had unsuccessfully predicted that the comet Halley's passage in 1987 would destroy the world, the date of March 26, 1997, came as a final day for followers of the Heaven's Gate sect. On the date, the Hale-Bopp Comet would pass near Earth. They understood that those who died on that day would continue to travel aboard that comet, and, with that, a large number of followers committed suicide.

**Bug**. And then it came the "millennium bug", the catastrophe that would occur on January 1, 2000, because of a change in the manner dates are recorded between the beginning of the computer age and the practice adopted at the end of the twentieth century.

Data from the 1950s and a few more years later were recorded with date that saved only the final two digits for the year. Instead of 1958, for example, 58 was written. With the turn of the millennium, this custom would bring serious problems, since the year 18 could refer to 1918 as well as to 2018. It was speculated that confusion could bring financial and even military catastrophes.

Banks, universities, governments and the military, among other institutions, have tried to review all the previous archives in order to adapt their dates to the demands of the new times.

There was nothing mystical about the millennium bug, but the dread of the most credulous at the end of 1999 was not much different from that of the Europeans in 999.

Moreover, although the millenarian seers had lost their strength throughout the twentieth century, one time lavish on materialism, there was an esoteric component at that date. Before treating it, however, it is advisable to take a walk through life and work of some emblematic figures of the second European millennium in this field of premonitions.

**Hildegard**. Mother Hildegard, canonized as St. Hildegard of Bingen and included in the list of the doctors of the Church by Pope Benedict XVI (in all of history there are 35 doctors of the Church, saints with a prominent doctrinal role, and four of them are women: St. Teresa of Avila, St. Catherine of Siena, St. Teresa of Lisieux and St. Hildegard of Bingen), was born in Rheinhessen, Rhine Valley (today in Rhineland-Palatinate), Germany, on September 16, 1098, and died at the Monastery of Rupertsberg, of Bingen, also in Rheinhessen, on September 17, 1179.

The prophetic work of this mother superior, Benedictine nun, enjoys little exposure in front of the set of her intellectual work, given the enormous scope and splendid significance of the whole. She wrote theological, cosmological and anthropological works, producing, among others, a book on natural sciences, called *Physica*; the first artificial language of history, which she called the *lingua ignota* (unknown language), what gave her the title of patroness of Esperantists in modern times; and the composition of at least 78 sacred songs, one of which was included in the soundtrack of the film "A beautiful mind", about the life of John Nash. An example of his musical work is "Ave generosa" (type in the browser window: **bit.ly/2Pq6ciW**).

Hildegard is known as the "Rhine Sibyl", or, as the Church

prefers, the "Teutonic Prophetess". Of noble family, she was the tenth child born of the pair Hildebert of Bermersheim and Matilde (Mechtild) of Merxheim-Nahet. Because she was a very sick girl, with little chance of growing up and becoming a mother of a family, and also being the tenth among the brothers, she was delivered early to the religious service as "tithing". Since she was a little girl, she used to have visions, "a light that made my soul tremble", she said, but she decided she would not tell anyone that because she was afraid of what they might think of her. This light that she saw presented images and colors, accompanied sometimes by voices, which commented on the meaning of visions, and also of music. His education was in charge of the Countess Judith von Spanheim (Jutta), who instructed her in the reading of Latin and the Bible, as well as the practice of Gregorian chant. They lived in the castle of the family of Judith until the age of fourteen of Hildegard, in 1112, when both gave themselves to the cloister, in the monastery of Disibodenberg, which, although being of monks men, created a wing of nuns, which happened to be directed by Judith herself. In 1114 that ward became an independent convent, given the large number of sisters it had added. In 1936, upon Judith's death, the nuns elected Hildegard as their new superior, unanimously.

In 1141, after turning 42, she had a vision accompanied by a voice that recommended that she should start writing about what she saw and heard. Since she was a good reader of Latin, but without the practice of writing in that language, she instituted as private secretary one of the monks of Disibodenberg, Friar Volmar, and turned into collaborator the young nun Richardis von Stade, very skilled in writing and who had with Hildegard a relationship almost from daughter to mother.

Still in doubt as to making public these reports, he consulted by letter Bishop Bernard of Clairvaux, later canonized as Saint Bernard, explaining his situation and asking for advice. He encouraged her and gave her support, which instigated her to continue. Pope Eugene III, Bernard's former pupil, was briefed on the case and also supported the work of the prophetess. He publicly read some excerpts from her texts at a synod in Trebevens, and declared that they were inspired by the Holy Spirit.

In 1151 she completed her first book, *Scivias* (contraction of *Scito Vias Domini*: Know the Paths of the Lord), in which she recounted her sensory experiences.

Before the conclusion of the book she had a vision in which she received the recommendation to transfer the nuns to a new convent, which she should found in Rupertsberg. The abbot of the monastery did not agree, saying that she was being carried away by vanity, which made her ill for a while, but with firm determination she faced all the inconveniences that got into the project and made the transfer, accompanied by twenty nuns. His main collaborator, Richardis von Stade, who was a Marquise, had dealt with the matter with the Archbishop of Mainz, Henry I, who gave the authorization.

In this new house, before even concluding Scivias, she wrote Physica, a book on natural medicine (*Cause et Cure*) and the work *Liber Vite Meritorum* (Book of the Meritorious Life). She also began composing her liturgical chants in the collection she called *Symphonie Armonie Celestium Revelationum*.

But, shortly after the installation of the new convent, and it was not clear where the idea had gone, the daughter of the heart, Richardis, was appointed superior mother of the Convent of Bassum in Saxony, having to leave Rupertsberg, against all the protests of Hildegard, who even appealed to the Pope, without success. A year later Richardis passed away.

Between 1163 and 1173 she wrote the *Liber Divinorum Operum* (Book of the Divine Works), the third of her great theological works. The long time spent is justified by her travels, which she did as a preacher.

In her preaching she emphasized conversion, salvation, the fight against corruption in the clergy, and the campaign against the Cathars, who embraced Gnosticism.

Of all the record of his prophecies, what counts most to us eight and a half centuries later is her vision of the Antichrist. The account is in the book Scivias and, since it was not of the profile of the Rhine Sibyl to enter in clash with the orthodoxy of the Church of Rome, what she did was to give details on that figure announced in the epistles of John the Evangelist. Since she is now considered to be one of the Doctors of the Church, what she wrote on the subject became official as the position of the Church itself.

Hildegard deals with the Antichrist also in the Liber Divinorum Operum, but only in passing, unlike what she does in the Scivias, in which she brings the details of the vision.

Scivias is divided into three parts, which are Creation, Redemption and Sanctification, respectively, the works of the Father, the Son and the Holy Spirit. Explanations of 26 visions are included in the book, each accompanied by an illustrative painting.

The image of the upper left corner of the Antichrist's painting depicts the five beasts, or beasts: an orange dog, representing the biting people; a yellow lion, who are aggressive people; a beige horse, representing those who insist on sin; a black pig, which are the lascivious people; and a gray wolf, who are deceitful individuals. Those beasts look to the west, where they see a hill with five peaks.

The upper right corner of the painting shows a building, which is the Church, and on it one sees the figure of Jesus Christ, resplendent, with open arms, dressed in purple and with a lyre on his knees. The feet, or shoes, are white as milk, representing the preservation of purity. At the bottom of the picture she depicted the church in the figure of a crowned woman, with a trunk full of scales, with open arms and also open hands. From her genitals appears the head of the Antichrist: eyes of fire, nose and face of lion and ears of ass, forming a dark being. From the knees to the heels, the woman's legs are full of blood. The meaning is that the Antichrist is born in the Church itself as a result of the sin that thrives within it. In front of this woman, the painting shows that the Antichrist tried to rise and reach the sky. There is a great noise, however, and he falls from the mountain in a filthy mist, frightening the people below, which asks for the protection of the heavens, and wonder why they are deceived. After that, the woman's feet become white, splendorous, "more than the sunshine".

According to Hildegard, the Antichrist convinces crowds, teaching that they have to give vent to their desires of riches and pleasures, they have to abandon vigils and fasts and only love the Lord, whom he claims to represent. He says that by doing this, people will be released from hell and reach the light, living with the Lord (the Antichrist) forever. He preaches your followers to make circumcision (in this we see something from the Benedictine orthodoxy of the prophetess), rejects baptism and the Gospel and relaxes all the severe precepts of Christian laws. He calls foolish all those people who, "through lies, established this observance for simple people".

According to the views of the Teutonic prophetess, the purpose of the Antichrist is to gain for himself the whole of humanity. And when will the birth and the fall of it be given? Only the Creator has the answer. The dates are not in her writings.

The reader can get a better understanding of Hildegard's life by watching Margarethe Von Trota's "*Vision - From the Life of Hildegard von Bingen*", 2009, with Barbara Sukowa.

**Mirabilis**. Roger Bacon, a Franciscan friar who was born in Ilchester, England, in 1220, and died at Oxford, in 1292, became known by his nickname *Doctor Mirabilis* (Admirable Doctor) for the depth of his studies, his knowledge and his intelligence. He was not a prophet who received visions of the future, but he anticipated, with the use of science, a great number of technological advances in the modern world. As with Leonardo Da Vinci three centuries later, many of the inventions he designed were only on paper, awaiting viability, since in his time there were no resources to implement the undertakings he imagined.

Religious and teacher, by profession, he did not discuss the end of the world, but he described machines that are an integral part of our time, which for many is the final stage for humanity. According to him, the development of the "experimental science", the expression he created, was the way in which we humans would help Jesus Christ to defeat the forces of backwardness and evilness, that is, the Antichrist.

Bacon joined Oxford University at the age of 13, and received a Bachelor of Arts degree, which was the name of the Mathematics course in the early centuries of the medieval university. Among his professors was Robert Grosseteste, Franciscan, first chancellor of the

Oxford University and later bishop of Lincoln. Grosseteste pioneered experimental studies of oblique throwing and defended the use of Mathematics as the basis of natural laws. According to him, for the origin of the universe, the Creator first established a small material point, making it emit light, and from there it came the creation of all the rest of the existing things. Such a view is considered by many to be the first, astonishingly precocious, proposal of the Big Bang theory. He also translated into Latin the "Nicomachean Ethics", by Aristotle.

It appears that Bacon's greatest influencer on the importance of experimentation, having Mathematics as its language, must have been Robert Grosseteste. Among the statements attributed to Bacon, one states: "Mathematics is the door and key to all sciences". Another says: "The abandonment of Mathematics brings damage to all knowledge, for whoever ignores it cannot know the other sciences or the things of this world".

In the Second Barons' War, this one against the royal house of Henry III, initiated in 1264 (the first, of 1215, was against John Lackland), his family took the party of the king, who was defeated. With this it came poverty, to his parents and to himself. Some biographers bet on the fact that he had a laboratory, with some inventions, whether in the Optics area or in the Mechanics area, and that this was lost in the fire of battle. The irony is that he was the first person in the West to develop a formula for gunpowder, which the Chinese had used for centuries to make fireworks. According to his explanation, that product, properly compressed, could cause great explosions. If the king had anticipated the use of gunpowder, he would certainly have been victorious.

Unlike Mother Hildegard, who criticized corruption in the Church without questioning the system itself, Roger Bacon was a severe critic of the curriculum and didactic method of Scholasticism, mainly because of the emphasis on pure theory, with contempt for practice. He said that if a young man were trained by that method in a country that did not know the fire, the first thing that would happen to him when traveling to an ordinary country would be to burn himself, once the fire was only known to him in theoretical form, which does not cause pain.

In the studies of Optics, Bacon explained the rainbow and perfected instruments, following the line of studies of al-Hazen. From the astronomical observation, he concluded that the Julian Calendar was wrong, since it accumulated lag of a few days in relation to the movement of translation of the Earth. He made the calculations for the correction, but these were only adopted in 1582, in the Gregorian Calendar, of Pope Gregory XIII, by the insistence of scientists of the University of Salamanca.

Because of his critical spirit, he raised many disagreements among the clergymen. When one of those who strongly disagreed with him became his hierarchical superior, he decided to move to France, where he continued his studies, and for ten years he was a professor at the University of Paris.

Cardinal Guy le Gros de Folques, with whom he became friends, liked his ideas and encouraged him to write them in form of book. He then began the production of his *Opus Majus*, an enormous compendium dealing with Mathematics, Physics, Logic, Ethics and Grammar, among other subjects. While he was developing this work, Folques became pope, with the name of Clement IV. In 1267 he sent the work to the Holy See, by a friar who assisted him, and shortly after that same year he sent another book, called *Opus Minus*, which was a new approach on the same themes, but more briefly. As his friends called this new book Opus Secundum, the next book he wrote was called *Opus Tertius*, and this one he also sent to the Pope, in 1268. Unfortunately, the pope died that year without having received the works that came from Paris on horseback. The next Pope, Gregory X, was not at all sympathetic to Bacon's ideas.

According to some biographies, he was imprisoned in Rome, between 1277 and 1279, on charges of heresy, but the story was never confirmed by the Church.

Among the inventions he described as possible through scientific advancement we may mention, for example, the steamboat, which, as we have seen above, was only built in 1803: "Boats may be moved without oars or rowers, so that large ships may be driven in the sea or in a river by a single man". At another time he imagined automobiles: "Cars can be built that will move without any animal traction at an incalculable speed". On air vehicles he proposed the hot-air balloon, "a large hollow ball of fine copper filled with liquid fire or air", which was only built in 1709, in Lisbon, by the Brazilian priest Bartolomeu de Gusmao, in the form of his famous "Passarola", although, even with the credit of the Church for Gusmao, until the moment the academia only recognizes like first flight the one of the brothers Montgolfier, in France, in 1783.

While using an idea similar to that advocated by Leonardo Da Vinci centuries later, he also wrote that "flying machines would be fabricated in which a man could sit and activate a certain mechanism of wings artificially constructed, like a bird in flight".

He also imagined the submarine: "Instruments can be made to walk in the sea, or in rivers, even in the bottom of them".

Having died unrecognized at the end of the thirteenth century, Roger Bacon's name gradually grew in history, especially at the hands of historians of science. Today there is a lunar crater with his name and there is also the asteroid Rogerbacon, the number 69,312, discovered in 1992.

**Shipton**. Ursula Southeil, of Knaresborough, Yorkshire, who lived from 1488 to 1561, was a prophetess who became known as Mother Shipton, after marrying carpenter Toby Shipton, in 1512.

It was only eighty years after she died that the first publication with her prophecies arose, so that between what she said and what came out printed there may have been much difference. In an 1862 edition came an end-time prediction: "The world to an end shall come / In eighteen hundred and eighty one". This obviously increased the fame of the seer, but a certain Charles Hindley confessed after he invented that couplet. In different versions, worldwide, the date was being adapted, the last being the year 1991. This is just a joke of people who want to win something using the name of seers who were worried about other things.

As we can see, this case of prophecy with a marked date is almost always the result of some manipulation, since the seer does not usually see dates.

Mother Shipton's predictions almost always dealt with local issues, about people in her neighborhood. It may, however, have come out of her pen a quatrain with predictions similar to Roger Bacon's technological prognostics: "A carriage without a horse shall go; / Disaster fill the world with woe... / In water iron then shall float, / As easy as a wooden boat".

It is said that Mother Shipton was born in a cave, which today has the name of Mother Shipton's Cave and is a place of public visitation.

**Bandarra**. Antonio Goncalves Annes de Bandarra, known as Shoemaker Bandarra, because of his profession, was a popular poet who wrote prophetic verses in his city of Trancoso, Portugal. He was born in the year 1500 and died in 1556. When in 1580 Portugal was absorbed by the Spanish crown, Bandarra gained renown because his verses seemed to predict the return of King Dom Sebastiao, who died young in battle in Africa in 1578, to conquer Morocco, and, without leaving any heirs, made his country lose autonomy two years later, after the death of an uncle who succeeded him and also had no children, once he was a cleric.

The Spanish Dominion over Portugal lasted 60 years, ending, then, in 1640. In the poems of Bandarra, interpreters understood an open scissors as the Roman number 10 (X). Closed scissors, number 2 (II). One of the blocks said, "Augury, people to come, / For the King, who will come here, /He will come again to ye, / As soon as past 30 scissors". The 30 scissors mean 30 times 2, which are those 60 years.

A few quartets, according to the reviewers, predicted the invasion of Portugal by the troops of Napoleon Bonaparte. The last of them says: "The name is of nine letters: / Two are of the same caste, / One should look how to spend it, / Not to perish by hunger". "Bonaparte" is the word of nine letters, two of them being "a".

Without referring to any date, other quartets seem to deal with World War II, like the following: "There will be along all Spain / neither privileged place; / everything will be ravaged / by these people from Germany ".

Some imagine, from some prophecies, that the "war" of the end of the world will come from the East to the West. Hence some interpreters from the Bandarra courts understand that this final battle deals with the next quartet: "From where the sun is rising / A Dragon I see arriving: / And its cable comes running / More animals come following".

In the days of the restoration of the crown, Bandarra inspired the prophetic writings of Father Antonio Vieyra. At the beginning of the twentieth century, Fernando Pessoa also took seriously his predictions regarding the fate of the Lusitanian culture.

By the content of his verses, he was accused by the Inquisition of "Judaizing" practices, receiving therefore a condemnation of the Holy Office. Bandarra had written that in the future Catholics and Jews would be united under the same religion. The penalty, however, was slight, and he was able to return to Trancoso and continue his work as a shoemaker.

As it was said above, the dates are not part of the visions of the prophets, and when it is said of seer A or B that predicted such an event for such a year, one must be wary of any manipulation. Of inscriptions on buildings of antiquity, for example, there are two emblematic cases. One is a Mayan monument on the Yucatan Peninsula, Mexico, indicating end of the world for the year 2012. Before the date, however, many already said that what was foreseen was a great transformation. Well, that would be valid for 2012, but also for any other year. Hieroglyphs are the other document in pyramids from Egypt, pointing to some twist at the height of the year 2000. We can see this in the same way that we are seeing the Mayan "prophecy". Only one of the known prophets was able to date some of his predictions, and we will see how this happened.

**Nostradamus**. The various dates set for the end since the year 1000 were anchored in the popular saying that decreed for the planet, addressing it, the following sentence: "By 1000 you know you'll pass, in 2000 you'll not arrive". Nostradamus, Dr. Michel de Notredame, the greatest of the prophets of Christendom, reinforced the belief in writing the 72nd court of his century X: "*Nineteen, nine, nine, seven months, / The great king of terror will come from heaven: / Resurrecting the king of Angoumois, / But before Mars the kingdom has a praise*".

If he had said 1999 more three times seven months, instead of adding only seven months, he would have hit the year and month of the overthrow of the Twin Towers in New York. As prophets see the future, perhaps through earthworm holes, but cannot pinpoint details of their vision, all clairvoyance is nebulous, and only after the prediction has been made, then, one understands what the persuader wanted to say.

Among the prophecies, the one that points to a date is even more dubious. The seer does not have a date-tracking system for the event he is anticipating, unless that date appears written next to the object of the vision, and it seems that this has never occurred.

The case of Nostradamus is distinct from the others because he coupled to his visions an astronomical configuration, which, for those who know the subject, means a date.

Born in Saint-Remy de Provence on December 14, 1503, Nostradamus entered the Medical School at the University of Montpellier after graduating from the University of Avignon. Approved in his credits in 1525, the university denied him the title of doctor after discovering that he was an apothecary, that is, was practicing pharmacology on his own.

Working as an apothecary, Nostradamus faced plague epidemics by presenting drugs that he himself developed. After losing his first wife to the plague, while he cared for the other patients, he settled in Salon-de-Provence. In this small town he was occupied in publishing an almanac with orientations for the farmers, when perceiving a high demand by this type of service. He perfected himself in weather forecasts, which he published as a differential in his almanac. It was from this practice that he came up with the idea of making other kinds of predictions.

He then became a seer who "saw" the astronomical conjunctions connected with the events he foretold.

In preventing the court on an accident that would kill King Henry II, what happened in a fair, playful fight, when the opponent's spear pierced an eye, leading him to death, Nostradamus was summoned to Paris and happened to be very respected in the royalty, becoming a great friend of the queen, Catherine de Medici.

Despite that quartet scheduled for the year 1999, Nostradamus predicted the end of time to a much later date. In the "Letter to My Son Caesar", he wrote that this event is to be given in the year 3797. For him, therefore, we will still have almost two millennia of life on this planet.

He died on July 2, 1566, by cardiac collapse.


**Vieyra**. Father Antonio Vieyra, a Jesuit who was born in Lisbon, Portugal, in 1608, and died in 1697 in Salvador, Bahia, Brazil, wrote among his many works three related to prophecies: the Fifth Empire, *Clavis Prophetorum* (an incomplete book) and History of the Future. His complete work was published in 2013, in a total of 30 volumes, with organization of the University of Lisbon.

He was not a prophet who had visions or premonitions, like Mother Hildegard or Nostradamus. What he did was a deduction job, like Roger Bacon's. The great difference in relation to the English friar was that he made his approximations of the future based on the scientific knowledge, centered in Mathematics, Optics, Mechanics and Alchemy, which was the Chemistry of the time, while Vieyra was based on the interpretation of History and biblical prophecies, seeking to unravel the political organization of the world in the future.

Antonio Vieyra's father, Cristovao Vieyra Ravasco, worked for the Portuguese navy and happened to serve as an Inquisition clerk, who transferred him to Salvador, Brazil, to assist the Tribunal of the Holy Office in the then colony. In 1608 he demanded his family to come from Lisbon, to live with him, so the boy Vieyra came to study in Brazil at the age of six.

Studying at the School of the Jesuits, until his pre-adolescence he was a "weak" student, i. e., he had great difficulty of learning. It should be remembered that until the beginning of the twentieth century, basic education was built almost exclusively on the work of memorizing contents, with little or no deduction of the ability of one or another student to present. At one moment, according to Vieyra himself, he felt a "crack" in his head and soon everything started to make sense. This episode and this moment happened to be called the "Vieyra snap". In reality, almost all schoolchildren go through their moment of "Vieyra snap", without realizing it, because few follow a personal growth curve that is always growing and without jumping.

In 1624, with the Dutch Invasion, he took refuge in the woods and from this phase it came the discovery of his vocation for missionary work with the natives. In 1627 he became professor of Rhetoric in Olinda, Pernambuco, but he did not stay long, returning to Salvador to continue his theological studies. In December 1634 he was ordained a priest.

A few years later there was an arduous dispute over power in the colony, between Dominicans, who were in charge of the Inquisition, and Jesuits, with their work of catechesis and literacy. The Dominicans were victorious over the dispute and Vieyra, who criticized discrimination against new Christians, the newly converted Jews to Catholicism, in front of the old Christians, happened to be seen as a defender of the Jews. Thus, in 1641, a year after the restoration of the Portuguese crown, he returned to Lisbon, becoming a diplomat. In Holland he negotiated the return of the captaincies of the Brazilian northeast to the Portuguese crown and in 1648 went to the Portuguese embassy in France.

In Portugal, Vieyra defended the permanence of the Jews in the country, rising against expulsion measures, arguing that this meant discarding the industrious spirit and ingenuity of the Hebrews, what would impoverish Portugal. That preaching caused much disagreement against him. At the end of 1652, he decided to return to Brazil, to work in Maranhao, where he arrived in January 1653. In Sao Luis, the capital, that year, he criticized the owners of the sugar industry with the First Sunday of Lent Sermon, condemning the slavery of the natives and seeking to convince the planters to grant them freedom.

The following year, 1654, he uttered in the same city the Sermon of Saint Anthony to the Pisces, dealing with the settlers' discord about the Jesuits' preaching for the freedom of the Indians. Three days later he traveled to Lisbon to ask King Joao IV for some edict to guarantee the natives. After a shipwreck that almost killed him in the Azores, followed by a plunder by Dutch corsairs, he arrived in Lisbon and was able to recover from Holland his papers that the looters had taken.

He returned to Maranhao, but his preaching in favor of the Indians generated a reaction that led him to return to Portugal in 1661. He was welcomed by the new queen, Luisa de Gusmao, but the following year she was overthrown and replaced by Alfonso VI, who did not accept his ideas. Because of his prophetic writings he was convicted by the Inquisition, charged with heresy, and held for almost three years until his pardon in 1668. The following year he moved to Rome, where he lived six years. He made representations against the Inquisition of Portugal and succeeded in having the papacy suspend the work of the Tribunal of the Holy Office for almost seven years in Portuguese lands, from 1675 to 1681.

Returning to Portugal he was involved in setbacks by defending the Jews whose policy of expulsion the Inquisition resumed. After many disappointments, he decided to return to Brazil, no longer to tread in his native land, Portugal, saying, as portrayed in the film "Word and Utopia", by Manoel de Oliveira: "This land does not deserve my bones".

His studies published in the prophetic books indicated that Portugal would occupy the position of Fifth Empire of world history. In those times, Portuguese Jesuits spread to America, Africa, India, China, Japan, and more. Portuguese navigators founded colonies in India, China and Africa, in addition to the largest, Brazil, which had been populated and catechized in America. Rivals in this trajectory were Spain and, with some effort, Holland, that had remained independent of the Spanish empire in those days. It is not difficult to understand that Vieyra's deduction made sense.

The idea came from Daniel's interpretation of the dream of Nebuchadnezzar II, in which a statue of gold, silver, bronze, and iron appeared. These metals would represent successive empires that would come to dominate the world, beginning with the one in which Daniel was. They would be Assyria, Persia, Greece and Rome. The Fifth Empire, in the interpretation of Vieyra, would be the domain of Christianity. The clay that covered the whole Earth after the statue was destroyed by the stone that descended without the aid of human hands and became a mountain represented Christianity spread throughout all nations. The leadership of this Fifth Empire would be in the hands of the Portuguese chief of State. To do so, the crown would have to be transferred to America, which meant making Brazil the seat of the kingdom.

As we know, only a century and a half later, the crown was transferred, in 1808, with Brazil leaving to be a monarchy at the end of the same century, in 1889, already with a crown separated from Portugal. So far, Vieyra's prophetic calculation has not yet materialized, or has been diluted in history.

While Vieyra was imprisoned by the Inquisition, a devastating event occurred to those who spread premonitions or prophecies obtained by other means: the French Academy of Sciences, in 1666, decided to withdraw Astrology completely from the role of the sciences, declaring it a mere belief. The measure was a sign that the Enlightenment was taking its place in history, gradually moving away to forgotten areas the knowledge based in feeling and religions.

The occupation of making prophecies only came back through practices that touch upon the scientific method. In the first half of the nineteenth century, the Scottish physician James Braid coined the term "hypnosis", giving an explanation for the phenomenon, in one of the searches for explaining cure by Mesmerization. Mesmerism is a trend that emerged from the practices of the Austrian physician Franz Mesmer, who came to Paris in the times of Louis XVI and Marie Antoinette, obtaining much success with his theory of the "animal magnetism", having as clients even the royal couple. According to him, one can heal another by using his personal magnetism, by laying on of hands, for example. The French Academy of Medicine classified Mesmerism as a type of charlatanism, but many saw cures and tried an acceptable explanation. One of them happened to be hypnotism.

**Cayce**. In the twentieth century perhaps the most notable seer was Edgar Cayce. Born in Hopkinsville, Kentucky, United States, on March 18, 1877, he died on January 3, 1945, in Virginia Beach, State of Virginia.

At the age of five Cayce was overthrown by a baseball bat and was taken to the hospital as if dead. But within minutes he woke up and apparently had no sequel, except perhaps the gift that was revealed later, which was to make predictions in a state of hypnosis.

He just completed high school, stopping from studying in order to work. His job of life was that of photographer, who in the late nineteenth and early twentieth century represented a good breadwinner, once few had a camera and still less a laboratory of developing negatives and printing portraits. His first job was as an insurance salesman, but he suffered a laryngitis that made him lose his voice. He chose the photograph, which allowed him to work without speaking. He belonged to the religion Disciples of Christ, from which he became a minister.

One day a hypnotist, known as Hart, came to his city, ensuring to promote healing for various ailments just by using hypnotism. Cayce wanted to try and was hypnotized, but remained mute. Another hypnotist, Al Layne, appeared later and, with this one, Cayce was able to speak during the hypnotic session. Still hypnotized, he made his own diagnosis. He was cured and, at the insistence of Al Layne, continued to repeat the sessions, in which he would present diagnosis and cure to others. One of Cayce's demands was that this work would have to be free.

In addition to diagnostics, it also revealed facts that would occur later. He then earned the nickname "sleeping prophet". Whenever he was going to be hypnotized, he asked persons to record what he said, so that he himself could hear his pronouncement. He never remembered what was said during the sessions.

There is the possibility that part of these Cayce hypnosis products was something similar to ordinary dreams, amid prophetic visions and clairvoyant descriptions. Sigmund Freud, who did not believe in premonition, understood, as was said above, that the unconscious could see through walls, such it is the power of this abstract apparatus.

Those who do not believe in this reach of the unconscious must reflect on an important episode in the history of the twentieth century. The Red Brigades (*Brigate Rosse*), a guerrilla group from Italy, abducted in December 1981 Brigadier General James L Dozier, a representative of the United States Army in NATO. Three years earlier this group had kidnapped and assassinated former premier Aldo Moro. The authorities' concern about the fate of the general was therefore very large and well founded. There were 42 days of searching and investigations, without much success, until the military's wife, perhaps an admirer of Edgar Cayce, proposed to undergo hypnosis as a means of helping with the work. The guerrillas had left her in the apartment in Padua when they took her husband. In the hypnosis session she described the captivity of the general, who was soon released, with the task force arresting all members of the terrorist cell that held him. On his return to the United States he personally received congratulations from President Ronald Reagan.

Other followers of Cayce obtained important results based on their example, unraveling mysteries, the main one being the diagnosis of diseases that medical examinations with conventional equipment did not detect.

The change of the seer to Virginia Beach occurred in 1925, after a hypnosis session arose the revelation that sands of that place were medicinal and that, therefore, there should be a hospital there that used this resource. For the project, he was funded by stockbroker Morton Blumenthall, an enthusiast of the sleeping prophet's jobs. In addition to the allopathic remedies indicated by the doctors to the patients, Cayce also recited hydrotherapy, physical exercises, massage and phytotherapy.

All was well there until the year 1929 approached. In one of the sessions, Cayce predicted the Great Depression, resulting from the general collapse of financial centers around the world, with its epicenter in New York. Blumenthall later asked if there would be something to be done to reverse the crisis. Cayce's response was that there would be no more timing.

Blumenthall was impoverished by the stock market crash and the hospital suffered the consequences of lack of money. Cayce then turned to esoteric investigations on past lives and, contrary to modern scientific understanding, on the value of astrology. To deepen this line of studies, in 1931 he founded the *Association for Research and Enlightenment* (A.R.E.), which since then has taken care of the documentation concerning his work and his career. This option for esotericism has led him to a kind of ostracism for more than a decade. The rumor that he was consulted, at different times, by Thomas Alva Edison and Nikolas Tesla, on questions of electricity and electromagnetism, has no confirmation in the records of his foundation, the A.R.E.

Finally, in 1943 he was hired by the government to, using his clairvoyant power under hypnosis, try to locate missing soldiers on the battlefield. While having obtained success in all the requested cases, he regained him reputation, being respected until the death, in 1945.

Some of Cayce's predictions were associated with dates, but, as stated above, without the view of an astronomical setting attached to fact, or without the view of a calendar, risking a date for an anticipated event in a premonition hardly ever proves to be a less nebulous information than the fact described. Between what the seer sees and what he interprets about what he saw there is a considerable distance, for he speaks with the language and concepts of his time. Imagine an eighteenth-century prophet describing a "digital photograph". The word "photography" still did not make sense, let alone the complete and more advanced concept, joining photography with computing. For all intents and purposes, what he could say is that he visualized a picture, or a very well painted picture. That is, if he saw the future, he could not convey what he envisioned.

In Cayce's predictions, two dates, in terms of years, were the most significant. According to him, a major transformation was to begin in the world in 1958, and the process would last until 1998. From then on, a new era would come.

We can speculate on this change that began in 1958. When Cayce passed away, the Von Neumann architecture computer was being built in Pennsylvania to be completed in 1946 (*Eniac* - Electronic Numeric Integrator And Computer) and it was only in the 1950s that it became a marketable item, with the 1958 *Univac* (Universal Automatic Computer) model. In 1957 a powerful and easy-to-use programming language, *Fortran* (Formula Translator), was released. The next year, 1958, another language even more malleable, designed to be taught in computer courses, won the world, *Algol* (Algorithmic Language). Still in 1958 the second generation of computers appeared, with machines based on transistors, no longer on valves, what reduced the size of the apparatuses and the energy expenditure. In 1959 a language created for commercial and banking purposes, *Cobol* (Common Business Oriented Language) was launched. Since then, the languages released have received only incremental advances, until the object programming (programming with little windows), in the early 1980s, as a development of the Simula 67 language, and, in the mid-1990s, Internet codes.

In 1998, the great novelty in technology was the launch of the Google search engine, which surpassed the AltaVista, 1995, very much used by those who started on the internet in the twentieth century. With Google, the practice of searching the Internet has become popular, not just for computer aficionados.

If the Cayce's vision has been about computing, the greatest hit of the date is at the end of the period, 1998, with the popularization of the Internet, because the onset of computing was already under way when he died. We can, relinquishing ill will, to consider that this revolution was the second-generation computer, a step that allowed, decades later, an ordinary citizen, even a preteen, to carry a computer in his pocket in the form of a smartphone.

Cayce, however, said that after this great transformation that the world would experience, there would be the beginning of geological changes previously unthinkable, unrelated, one can deduce, to human technological advances. The Earth's magnetic poles will leave their positions, he said. This will lead to great cataclysms. Regions previously icy will become hot, and vice versa. Floods, earthquakes, tornadoes, volcanoes will all occur frequently. Countries will lose considerable parts of their territories, which will be submerged. The city of New York will disappear, being rebuilt later in another area, whereas Japan almost entirely will be swallowed by the waters of the sea. New territories will emerge from the oceans, including the lost continent of Atlantis. The great California earthquake, expected because of the San Andres Fault, will finally occur. South America will also suffer great shocks and the Antarctic, thawed in its northern part, will show new lands, with rivers running over them, near Tierra del Fuego. One of the safest states in Europe will be Ireland, which will suffer much fewer shocks than its neighboring England.

Once the Earth is finally adapted to the new location of the magnetic poles, everything will calm down. The planet will not suffer any more volcanoes, or hurricanes, or earthquakes, or tsunamis. Perhaps there, something he has not said, nor could have said, tectonic plates are well fitted, without the flaws and gaps that terrified the Earthmen decades ago, since the problem was detected and known, from the proposition of Harry H Hess, Princeton University, 1962. It is the geological explanation, found for the Alfred Wegener's theory of "continental drift", in 1915, that continents are not fixed in the earth's crust, but glide slowly and permanently.

In these boom times, the population of Russia will teach the rest of the world how to live the human fraternity and true freedom that they have developed there, not by inheritance of Bolshevism, but as a result of their culture.

Cayce, living up to the fame of the greatest prophet of the twentieth century, saw not only the present and the future, but also the remote past. Atlantis, a continent that Plato claimed to have existed west of the Strait of Gibraltar, having submerged many centuries before the formation of the Hellenistic civilization, appeared in the visions of the sleeping prophet as a place that paid for the errors of its own inhabitants, who advanced too much in knowledge and techniques, but they did not have full control of the forces they manipulated. The Atlanteans explored the power of crystals in matters of healing and energy, and dominated telepathic communications. Before submersion, they split into two antagonistic currents, one that sought to use technological advances to regain links with nature and to help one another, while another preferred to rely on material goods without humanitarian concerns. They ended in a war whose outcome precipitated the sinking of the continent. Some of those inhabitants used their foresight to assess the risks and escape in a timely manner, electing Egypt as their destination. They taught the Egyptians many of the knowledge that only Atlantis possessed at the time.

About predictions, Cayce cautiously asserted that nobody could accurately explain events from the distant future.

**Vanga**. Vangelia Pandeva Dimitrova, known as Baba Vanga, named Vangelia Gushterova after marriage, was born in the Ottoman Empire, the town of Strumica, today belonging to Northern Macedonia, on 31 January, 1911, and died on 11 August 1996 in Sofia, Bulgaria, country that she has adopted to live since young.

It is considered one of the greatest seers of the twentieth century, perhaps losing in prestige in the area only for Edgar Cayce. Like the American, she also went through a kind of Near-Death Experience (NDE) in adolescence. Living in Serbia, where her father moved, after serving in World War I and becoming a widower, she was once picked up by a hurricane that carried her for two kilometers. Found by neighbors, her eyes were filled with sand and she could not open them because of the pain. She survived the accident but became blind and never recovered sight.

Still in Serbia, he joined a blind school in Zemun in 1925, where he learned the Braille alphabet, riding, playing the piano, and cooking.

Without seeing through the eyes, he realized that he possessed the gift of clairvoyance, seeing facts that others could not perceive, including premonitions about events in the short and medium terms. His father had arranged a new wife, but this one also died, while Vangelia studied in the special school. She then had to stop her studies to go back to the house and take care of her brothers.

With the brothers now grown, one day one of them, Vasil, wanted to go to a party and she cried a lot, begging him to give up, because something very serious would happen. He paid no attention and left. He was later found dead, his body bruised and shot.

Another coincidence with Cayce was that she was able to make correct diagnoses and prescribe effective medical herbs to sick people who sought her. And during World War II, he accurately visualized the location of missing soldiers. As a result of World War I, her hometown had become part of Bulgaria, so she became officially Bulgarian. In recognition of this work of locating soldiers, on April 8, 1943, she was visited by the Bulgarian emperor, Czar Boris III.

Scholars of paranormal affairs wrote that she predicted, among other things, World War II, the fall of the Soviet Union and the Chernobyl nuclear disaster.

In 1994 she predicted that the final match of the World Cup would be played between two teams with initial "B". They immediately deduced that it would be Brazil and Bulgaria, and the Bulgarians began to celebrate in advance. But it was only half of the forecast, for the final was between Brazil and Italy, with victory of the first, on penalties.

It was repeatedly reported on the Internet at the beginning of the 21st century that she had foreseen World War III, which began with the use of nuclear artifacts, as dated to the year 2010, lasting three or four years. As nothing similar happened, close relatives and friends were consulted in Bulgaria. The answer was that she made no such predictions.

Huge calendars circulate today with predictions of Baba Vanga year by year, until the year 5079, when the world and the universe would end. These prophecies are all, however, as valid as the outbreak of World War III in 2010. They are only inventions of playfulness.

# Chapter 7 - Difficulties in the application of science

**Formulas**. Stephen Hawking made prognoses based on the science of his time, just as Roger Bacon also did in his day. When we use science to predict a result whose paths we already know, there is almost certainty that we are not lying. In the hand of someone who knows how to scratch a match, we can guarantee with 100% certainty, minus an almost negligible epsilon of possibility of failure, which, if scratched, it will produce fire. If our calculations are correct, our formulas will almost certainly work for the first time. That is what happened to Roger Bacon when he created his European gunpowder formula. The idea was that, inflamed, it would cause the fire to spread in a flaming bonfire. If the first attempt failed, by mistake in the formula, this he did not report, but if there was an error, it was only because the calculation was incorrect earlier.

**Heights**. When it comes to applying science in a technological enterprise that involves many variables, it is difficult to get everything right in order to obtain the expected result in the first attempt. That is why the Russians, before sending the aeronaut Yuri Gagarin to circumnavigate the Earth through the outer space, sent the bitch Laika, who, by the way, died during the mission. Gagarin also died in flight, but piloting his airplane in regular military activity, not above the atmosphere, and only recently, in the XXI century, it was verified that the cause was depressurization.

**Glass**. Instigated by a patent that was registered in the United States in 1902 - in that country one allows to register patent only with the description of the product, without presentation of the prototype -, Alaistair Pilkington began in England in 1953 the production of float glass, that would be a form very cheap to get the flat glass directly from the oven, from the liquid glass. This liquid glass would be poured over a layer of tin and, with cooling, it would emerge completely flat and smooth. He invested almost all of the family's capital in this renewal, which would take the glass industry out of a process that came from Ancient Egypt. Well, the first attempt was a failure. All glass used in the test was lost because it did not release from the tin. Only after many adjustments, carried out by Pilkington and his partner Kenneth Bickerstaff, the project happened to work, four years later, with a lot of sweat poured and many nights of sleep lost.

**Alcohol**. Another similar case occurred with the use of alcohol fuel in automobiles. With the 1973 Oil Crisis, the Brazilian government decided to finance studies to introduce ethanol from sugarcane as a substitute for gasoline. In 1975 the government program called Pro-alcohol was launched, supporting physicist Jose Walter Bautista Vidal and engineer Urbano Ernesto Stumpf in the development of the alcohol engine for cars. The Institute of Technological Research (IPT), the Faculty of Economics and Administration of the University of Sao Paulo (FEA-USP), the Polytechnic School of the University of Sao Paulo and other university institutions were involved for a number of years. Because there was necessity of creating a new energy base, spread throughout Brazil. When the first cars were launched, running only with alcohol, everything seemed to go well, but months later winter came. The engines did not pick up. Some worked after half an hour of trying, others did not spin. In a first moment a system was developed that used gasoline for the ignition, which bypassed the problem. The irony is that it was later revealed that Henry Ford had patented the alcohol engine in the United States 70 years earlier and preferred to work with the gasoline engine. Perhaps he has seen the difficulty of using alcohol to reach that preference. And one of the difficulties, besides the operation issue, was the low supply of the product.

**Computation**. There are many examples showing that, by applying in practice a new scientific concept for the first time, we find that some item has been forgotten or that some calculation was wrong. More painful still is when an essential element for the realization of the product has not yet been reached, as it happened in the history of the computer.

In 1833, after completing the assembly of his Engine of

Differences, a very powerful calculator begun in 1922, the English industrialist Charles Babbage designed the grandfather of the modern computers, the Analytical Machine, with all the components of these machines, including a printer as a unit of output. The calculators that Babbage produced at his factory, performing addition, subtraction, multiplication, and division operations, were an invention of Leibniz, who perfected Pascal's calculating machine, which he simply added and subtracted. As a respected entrepreneur, Babbage secured government funding, and remained for years in the work of building his great machine. In 1871, the year of his death, a part of the apparatus was presented, with some functioning, not very distant of what already did the Engineer of Differences. The great gain in this trajectory was that her pupil and admirer, Ada Byron, countess of Lovelace, developed the steps to make the machine obey the programmer, i. e., to the individual who would feed with data, if it were built according to the original plan. This woman, daughter of the poet Lord Byron, died of uterine cancer at 36 years of age, is considered the inventor of computer programming.

Babbage missed two central scientific breakthroughs in computer construction. One was already available, which was Binary Arithmetic, created by Leibniz. Both Leibniz and he used Decimal Arithmetic on their machines. The other major breakthrough only came in 1886: the conception of making electrical or electronic circuits respond to the connectives of the Boolean Algebra, which are the OR, the AND, the NOT, the exclusive OR, and so on. With this feature is that the computer could make decisions, as was intended by Charles Babbage and Ada Byron. It was Charles Sanders Peirce, son of mathematician Benjamin Peirce, in the United States, who published an article bringing this innovation. He, however, wrote that he could not discern in what kind of activity his discovery could be used. Then Claude Elwood Shannon, Professor of Electrical Engineering at MIT (Massachussets Institute of Technology), presented in 1937 his master's thesis on applications of Logic, pointing the way to its use in computers. At that time, Herman Hollerith's machine, which was launched in 1896, and processed information from the reading of punch cards, developed from

Babbage's inventions, was already widespread in the US market, sold by Hollerith's company Computing Tabulating Recording Corporation, which later changed its name to IBM (International Business Machines).

If one leg was the electronic use of the Aristotelian Logic, also called Binary Logic, transformed into Algebra by George Boole in 1847, the other was in Leibniz's Binary Arithmetic, and the one who applied by the first time in a computer was the German engineer Konrad Zuse, who worked for Ford in his country. In 1934 he started building his machine, which he called Z1, and was smaller than a grand piano. It was still the presidency of Hindenburg, but soon his death came and Hitler became absolute chief. Zuse tried financing to market his machine and was unsuccessful. Nevertheless, he later built the successor machines, Z2, Z3 and Z4. With the theoretical work of Claude Shannon and the machine of engineer Zuse, professors J. Presper Eckert and John Mauchly completed in the University of Pennsylvania in 1946 the computer Eniac, the first one of Von Neumann architecture, that is the one that we use today even in the cellphones intelligent. It is called Von Neumann architecture because it was the Hungarian engineer John Von Neumann who published, shortly before, in the United States, the concept of the modern computer.

We see that what we perceive ahead of us when we possess recent scientific concepts that we intend to apply hardly takes place without deviations, stumbling and delays. We think we already have everything to visualize the facts as they will occur, but this is just an illusion. Yes, science gives us assurances, but we need to take the path to know that our predictions are almost always nebulous. If it is so with science, with the futurology of the prophets the wheat is much more difficult to visualize than the tares.

## Chapter 8 - Important physical phenomena

**Fundamentals**. Physics, today an independent science, was, until the middle of the nineteenth century, the part of Mathematics that dealt with the study of inorganic nature, through Kinematics, Dynamics, Electricity, Hydrology, Thermology, Wave Mechanics, Acoustics and other related areas. Thus, when the ancient people spoke of the importance of Mathematics to understand the world, the scope of the idea was greater than it is today, for the first thought was in Physics. The value of Mathematics did not decline because it grew too much and had to deal only with the field that is now called "Pure Mathematics", which does not deal with time-bound situations, but someone who wants to go deeper in the study of nature must today choose not Mathematics, but Physics, although it cannot do without the mathematical base.

In order to begin the discussion of the theme, we shall first move quickly through the three basic laws defined in the book *Principia* (Philosophiae Naturalis Principia Mathematica), by Isaac Newton, published on July 5, 1686. In these laws Newton departed from Galileo's Principle of Inertia and added two new ones. The three laws are as follows. I) First Law or Principle of Inertia: A body at rest tends to remain at rest, and a body in motion tends to remain in motion. II) Second Law or Fundamental Principle: The force is directly proportional to the product of the acceleration of the body by its mass, i. e., Force (**F**) is equal to mass (**m**) multiplied by acceleration (**a**). III) Third Law or Principle of Action and Reaction: For every force of action there is a reaction, with equal intensity, but in the opposite direction.

The Third Law is the best known and cited, because many imagine that they have already discovered how to apply it in open situations, in which many variables act, as is the case of social facts. It is necessary to take into account that in Newtonian Mechanics there is a situation of *Ceteris Paribus* ("all the more constant"), which is what allows us to make the necessary measurements for the calculations.

In any case, it is comfortable to know and understand some

central physical phenomena, so that we can have an idea of what path the world is taking. They are absolutely natural phenomena, but they can, in most cases, be activated by the human hand.

**Convection**. The first of these actions we are going to analyze is the *convection*, which has a very close relation to global warming. If the reader has studied it well, perhaps here he will find a new aspect of the question, and he may also have the opportunity to remember the theme.

Convection is one of three forms of heat transfer. The other two are *radiation* and *conduction*. Convection is defined as the transport of heat between two regions of a vessel, or an environment, through a fluid (liquid, gas or plasma), from the hottest to the coldest, or vice versa.

Everyone knows that if we try to heat water in a pan without a lid we will spend more time than in a covered pan. In both cases there is convection, but in the covered pan we control the heat flow inside a smaller volume, which also causes the transfers to occur in smaller time intervals. The region that first received heat, below, transfers the incoming heat to the uppermost region, which is cold, and when this cooler mass falls below it is heated and pushed upwards, repeating this movement until the temperature of the liquid pass through the boiling point, and keep increasing.

If we want to light a fire quickly, the most appropriate method is to create a hollow region in the middle of the coal, or in the middle of the wood, and, taking the flame to pieces of paper or other easily combustible material, inside that hollow, to wait up that the convection takes care of the rest. For example, with charcoal, we wrapped a bottle with old newspaper and put the charcoal around it. Then we removed the bottle leaving the cylinder formed by the newspaper, surrounded by coal, underneath. We now lit the paper and in less than a minute the coal will be burning.

In the terrestrial atmosphere convection heat transfer occurs continuously. We all know that the thermal radiation coming from the Sun, which is at a temperature of approximately 6,300° C, heats solid surfaces with greater intensity than liquid or gaseous regions. And the surface of the water holds more heat than the atmospheric air. It is said that under very hot sun it is possible to fry the egg on the surface of a stone. Thus, the surface of the soil and the ocean transmits heat through the water vapor that wanders through the atmosphere, especially on the seas. The heat rises and the water vapor forms the clouds, which can rise to a height of up to 14 km. At the top, compared to the temperature at the lower end, it suffers sudden cooling. Depending on the winds, which also act according to the convection, the cooling can cause the clouds to precipitate like drops of water or like acorns of ice, which are hail.

If the human action is sufficient to alter the flow of heat in the atmosphere, we automatically interfere with the volume and frequency of the rains.

The transfer of heat by radiation, the thermal radiation, occurs by the electromagnetic waves that all the bodies emit. As for the transfer by conduction, it works through direct contact between two bodies with different temperatures.

The amount of heat **Q** transferred, by time interval **t**, is given by the cooling formula, by Isaac Newton, which equals the ratio $dQ/dt$ to the expression $h*A(Ts-Ti)$, where **h** is the cooling coefficient, **A** the area in contact with the fluid, **T**s the temperature of the upper part of the vessel and **T**i the temperature of the lower part (the letter d before Q and t means infinitesimal difference, or differential). Heat (Q) and temperature (T) are distinct entities, as seen in the formula. Heat is one of the forms of energy, while temperature is the measure of the property of heating or cooling a body. In the International System of Units, heat is measured in joules (J) and temperature is given in degrees Celsius (°C).

**Dissipation**. The Second Law of Thermodynamics assures us that no thermal machine can take advantage of 100% of the energy supplied to it. There will always be some loss, which we call *dissipation*. The part taken is called yield.

If this limitation did not exist, perhaps the problem of global warming would be seen as a treasure for the industry, once we would have huge amounts of thermal energy to use without losing anything. It happens that if someone discovered this machine with 100% of income would be creating the "perpetual motion", which the Second Law says to be impossible.

Strictly speaking, every dynamic system, that is, every system that evolves in time, suffers energy dissipation. Regardless of the form of energy we use, the unused portion is dissipated as heat. For example, a rock that rolls downhill, moved only by mechanical energy, will lose acceleration upon reaching the horizontal part of the trajectory, and will decrease its acceleration until it stops. It stops by the action of friction, contrary to the sense of force that dragged it up there, and in friction there is loss of energy, which is heat and nothing more. A lighted filament lamp works by presenting light energy, but much of that energy is dissipated, heating the environment. Also a battery, from which we demand electricity through its chemical energy, produces heating as a result of its use.

To the three Laws of Thermodynamics, which arose from the work of the French theoretician Sadi Carnot, of 1824, on thermal machines, a Zero Law was added, which reads as follows: If two systems are in thermal equilibrium in relation to a third one (a thermometer to a given measure, for example), then they are in thermal equilibrium with each other.

The other three laws have the formulations that follow. I) An isolated system can exchange energy with the surrounding environment, in the form of work and heat, and accumulate internal energy. II) It is impossible to exist a process whose unique result is the transfer of heat from a body of lower temperature to one of higher temperature, from which it is deduced that the entropy (degree of disorganization) of the universe always tends to increase. III) The entropy of a system tends to a constant maximum value, just as the temperature tends to absolute zero (-273,15°C). The concept of entropy was introduced in the 1850s by Rudolf Clausius, a German physicist, and his mathematical description in terms of probabilities was provided in 1877 by Ludwig Boltzman, an Austrian. Entropy, which in Greek means "transformation", measures the irreversibility of dynamic systems.

**Expansion**. A very expensive concept for engineers, especially civil engineers, is the thermal expansion, a name given to the increase in volume of bodies as a result of the increase in temperature. When constructing a bridge or a large building, the engineer shall design some gaps, spans between component parts of the structure, with the measures necessary to expand the material according to the heating to which it may be subjected.

Expansion occurs in the heated body because they increase the intensity and frequency of the vibrations of their particles, which necessitates more space. In the case of fluids, such as gases and liquids, there is a tendency to the leaking of part of the substance, as in the case of milk when it reaches the boiling point. If we are not around to lower the fire in a timely manner, we will surely lose a portion of the product.

Thermal expansion always occurs in the three spatial dimensions of the body, i. e., in width, length and height. In the case of solids, it is possible to calculate how much will increase for each dimension, from the coefficient of expansion of the substance in question. The coefficient of linear expansion is the average increase in length that the substance presents for each increase of 1°C in its temperature. The coefficient of surface expansion is simply twice that of linear, while that of volumetric expansion is the triple.

The linear coefficient of iron, for example, is 0.000012/1°C. This means that if the iron bar is measured in centimeters, for each heating degree Celsius the bar will increase by 0.000012 cm. Other widely used coefficients are gold, 0.000014/1°C, and lead, 0.000029/1°C.

After a certain heating, the length L of a solid is given by $L_o(1+\alpha{*}\Delta T)$, that is, the new size is the initial length $L_o$ (multiplied by 1) added to the product of that length by the coefficient $\alpha$ and by temperature variation $\Delta T$. If we want to calculate the cubic variation, we adapt the formula, by substituting L for length by V for volume and $\alpha$ for linear expansion by $\gamma$ (gama) for volumetric, or cubic, expansion. To increase in area we change L by S and $\alpha$ by $\beta$.

For liquids, calculations are usually made for volumetric expansion, since it does not make much sense to speak, for example, in a linear meter or square meter of water.

Water, which is the major concern when it comes to global warming, has volumetric expansion coefficient of 0.00021/1°C, which means that if we considered linear expansion the coefficient would be 0.00007/1°C, approximately one quarter of the expansion of lead. We must also take into account the so-called "anomalous behavior of water", according to which, by experimental observations, between 0°C and 4°C the volume decreases instead of increasing as with other substances. The higher density of the water therefore occurs at a temperature of 4°C, from which it decreases and the volume increases again.

A monstrous tragedy for warming of the ocean water would come if this heating occurred from the bottom of the seas, because, in this case, the convection would also heat the entire mass of water and its volume would increase globally, flooding and destroying coastal cities around the world. Fortunately, it's not what we'd expect. We must remain vigilant in relation to the warming of the atmospheric air, since in the anthropogenic case it is made from the surface of the Earth from the bottom upwards.

On the expansion and compression of the air, we can not fail to mention the figure of Ctesibius, born in 285 BC and died in 222 BC, leader of the Mechanics School of Alexandria, also called the Mechanical School, which dilutes its meaning somewhat, or School of Engineers, which improperly anticipates the advent of Engineering in history (the first School of Engineering is the School of Bridges and Roads, Paris, 1747, which later became the Polytechnic School). Ctesibius, who created the first hair salon in history and worked there as a barber (some say the barber shop was his father's), was one of the greatest inventors of Antiquity, but with very little recognition. Among his creations are clepsydra, hydraulic clock with pointer, pressure pump, or suction pump, and also the musical instrument known as hydraulic tube organ. His discovery of the compressed air motor role represented for Antiquity a revolution almost as great as that of the use of electricity in modern times.

It should be noted, however, that the mechanism of air compression was based on the use of pressure, not on cooling or heating, although the role of temperature in the expansion of fluids was also known to the Alexandrines. A piston, moving in an air tube, or in a syringe, produces variation both in pressure and temperature of the fluid, so that the two measurements are mathematically related. One of Ctesibius's successors at the Mechanics School, Hero, who lived from 10 AD to 70 AD, is responsible for about 80 inventions based on compressed air, hydraulic pressure, or steam power, such as aeolipile, which he created inspired by Vitruvius idea.

One of Hero's famous inventions was a mechanism to automatically open the door of the temple, much earlier than the application of the photoelectric effect to open doors in the twentieth century. The priest lit a fire, which warmed a tank containing water, and this, increasing the pressure of the air, gave off a weight tied to a rope, which pulled the door. Among the many fun Hero inventions, such as an automatic puppet theater, or mechanical birds singing alone, there were also several utilitarian products, such as a fire-extinguishing pump.

**Resonance**. Ancient scholars have failed to decipher the mechanism of resonance, but by some accounts one realizes that the power of its action was known here or there. For physicists, it is only a matter of "resonance", but today the nomenclature "mechanical resonance" has been established to distinguish it from some of its many unfoldings, such as magnetic resonance, optical resonance, molecular resonance, orbital astronomical resonance, and others.

The resonance is a phenomenon studied within the theme Ondulatory, because it occurs as a manifestation of frequencies, amplitudes and length of waves. The name refers to one of the wave types, which is the sound wave, or acoustic. Let us think of two people side by side shaking rhythmically each of them a rope stretched ahead. The two strings tend to form pulses of waves. If these pulses, counting between peak and valley of each, have equal lengths (wavelengths) and disagree in their movement, being in the valley the wave of a rope in the moment in which the wave of the other, at the same distance of the hand of the activator, is at the peak, we will have a case of wave destruction, assuming that they can act together. We say that there is destructive interference. One pulse would obviously nullify the corresponding pulse of the other rope, since when one tries to ascend the other tries to descend. Now imagine that peaks and valleys of one rope coincide with peaks and valleys of the other, at the corresponding distances. If we can join the two movements into one, what we will observe will be an increase in amplitude (measure of height observed between valley and peak), even a doubling, if other forces do not interfere. We have constructive interference here. This increase in wave height when they add up is what we call resonance.

The velocity **v** of the wave pulse is the value of $\lambda$ (lambda), wavelength, divided by the period **T**, which is the time spent by the pulse to travel this length. Since the frequency **f** is the inverse of the period, we have that the velocity v is given by the product $\lambda*f$.

Every system has a natural frequency of oscillation. If we are to join two distinct systems, we must check whether the frequencies will not coincide, or we can cause great havoc. Each type of soil on which we build a house, for example, has its natural frequency. The engineer must know it, before designing the building. On a road where many trucks transit, the ground has its natural frequency adapted to the contact of the trucks as they pass over it. In this case, it is not enough to take into account only the natural frequency of the ground, but also the frequency adapted from the set solo more trucks. The trepidation of the terrain, which we can feel on our feet, or in our hands, can activate constructive interference in the coincident frequency waves in some construction alongside the road, knocking it down, with greater risk for recent works. The shock that comes from this situation is called "fluttering", which many deny is a case of resonance. However, it is only a special case of the phenomenon.

It is known the case of singers who adjust their soprano voice to break crystals. This occurs when the singer can match the frequency of her voice to that of the object.

In Antiquity the case of the "trumpets of Jericho" from the year 1400 BC is reported in the Book of Joshua, in the Bible, in which the Israelites were instructed to blow trumpets and shout to make the wall fall, in what they succeeded.

In the twentieth century, the most publicized fact on the subject was the fall of the Tacoma Bridge, in the State of Washington,

United States. Inaugurated on July 1, 1940, months later this suspension bridge began to rock. On November 7 of the same year she collapsed. Used since then in textbooks as an example of a disaster by resonance, in recent times experts have questioned the interpretation, explaining that the shaking was provoked by the winds, which produced "fluttering". The winds, certainly, may have helped the bridge to resonate with the environment. This was also the case in an evangelical church just opened in 1998 in Osasco, Brazil. On a given day the faithful decided to accompany the hymns by beating rhythmically with their feet on the floor, and the ceiling of the building came down. In this case it was not the wind, but the foot strokes that helped the resonance to take action.

There is an report that enters the account of legend, but that may be true, about the crossing of Napoleon's troops on a bridge. Rhythmically marching, the troops made the bridge shake and then collapse. From that day, every bridge crossing began to be made with the soldiers marching in disarranged footsteps. No more rhythm!

The great inventor Nikola Tesla, whose best known creations are the neon lamp and the radio (which is no longer attributed to Marconi), guaranteed that he had invented in 1898 a machine to produce earthquakes. It was a device that detected the natural oscillation of a body and began to vibrate at the same frequency. Making metal bars resonate in his laboratory, he startled neighbors, who called the police. Tesla then picked up a hammer and destroyed the machine. There is no proof that Tesla has really built this machine, but the story is not unlikely. The researchers do not believe, however, that the device could break the Earth into two pieces, "like an apple", according to what Tesla said.

Great natural disasters may have happened because of resonance. And it is not unthinkable for any tyrant to summon his scientists to create a powerful weapon based on this principle.

Magnetic resonance imaging, used in hospitals, has saved many people's lives. But we must not forget that resonance itself is a resource that can carry a great power of destruction, perhaps greater than the power of nuclear bombs, although the ways of manipulating it are not yet known.

**Radioactivity**. Since the atomic explosions in Japan in August 1945, determined by the Pentagon, the United States General Staff, radioactivity has become the most frightening physical phenomenon among all those who can be manipulated by the human hand. To complete the picture, we had the Chernobyl Nuclear Power Plant disaster on April 26, 1986, due to two explosions in a generator caused by overheating of the fuel. This is considered to be the greatest nuclear accident in history, which should serve as a tragic lesson so that no other will occur in those dimensions. So much so that the second most serious accident in this line, that of the Fukushima I Nuclear Power Plant in Japan, on March 11, 2011, due to a spill caused by a strong earthquake, had a very small number of victims, compared to that of the accident in Ukraine, because the public authority of Japan is highly equipped to minimize the damage resulting from such an occurrence.

In the Chernobyl accident the immediate victims, in a total of 31 dead, were the employees of the plant, followed by the first firemen to arrive, who suffered heavy contamination and soon died. Their bodies, in cement coffers, are buried in Moscow, once at that time Ukraine belonged to the Soviet Union, which had Moscow as its capital. At least 600,000 people were affected by radiation, not only in Ukraine, but also in neighboring Belarus and Russia. Many of those affected were sent to Cuba for skin treatment, because Cuba developed efficient methods in this area. Of the many people who have been dying in the years to come, from cancer or other illnesses, it is impossible to know how many and who have died because of the disaster.

One of the consequences of the Chernobyl disaster was the slowdown in investment in new nuclear fission power plants in various parts of the world. However great the precautions taken in setting up and operating the plants, the risks are too great to ignore voices advocating other, even more expensive, forms of energy generation. If there is a theocratic republic (Iran) and a family dictatorship (North Korea) insisting on nuclear expansion, this only shows that the human species is still far from making reason prevail in every corner.

The very discovery of radioactivity in 1896 was accidental, albeit without tragedy. Physicist Antoine Henri Becquerel had been studying in his laboratory in Paris the fluorescence of double sulfate of uranium and potassium. At one point he noticed that the uranium emitted a mysterious, unexpected radiation.

In 1895, the German engineer Wilhelm Conrad Roentgen experimented with fluorescent lights produced by electrons and placed them on a metal plate. One day he realized that luminescence struck the plate even when theoretically the electrons could not reach it. He interposed a screen between the tube that emitted electrons and the metal plate and saw that the luminescence still reached the plate. He then placed his own hand and saw her skeleton reflected on the plate, discovering then the discharge of electrons that, for lack of a better name, called X-rays.

Uranium had been discovered in 1789 by German researcher Martin Heinrich Klaproth, who extracted it as a black powder from the mineral known as plechblende. He named this new element in honor of the newly discovered planet Uranus. In 1818, the Swedish chemist Joens Jakob Berzelius extracted another new element, the thorium, from that ore. They did not suspect that these elements had this property of radiation, which Becquerel would discover.

What Becquerel realized was that uranium and potassium salt left stains on a photographic plate wrapped in black paper, as if there had been an X-ray discharge. He saw that when the amount of uranium increased, photographic printing increased. He realized that the phenomenon was not chemical, but purely physical, and gave it the name of "uranic emanations".

The couple Pierre and Marie Curie, close colleagues of Becquerel, as soon as they saw the publication of this one on the discovery made on the uranium, decided to deepen investigations in this field. In a short time, Marie Curie discovered that the thorium also emitted such "emanations". In 1898, studying the plechblende, she noticed that even after the extraction of the uranium contained in it, the "emanations" continued. Then she and Pierre isolated another element of that mineral, and gave it the name of "polonium", in homage to Poland, country of origin of Marie. That same year, she noticed that after extracting uranium and polonium from the plechblende, there was still some material that produced "emanations". Then she extracted another element, the "radio". The name "radiation" was then consolidated for this strange activity of these elements, and this field of study came to be called Radioactivity.

Five years later, in 1903, Becquerel, Pierre Curie and Marie Curie shared the Nobel Prize in Physics for those discoveries and the development of this new field of research.

In 1906 Pierre Curie died in an accident in which he was run over by a carriage. Madame Curie, his wife, became his successor in the chair he had been occupying at the Sorbonne, currently the University of Paris VI. She was the first woman to receive a science chair in that institution. In 1910 she published her research in the book *Treaty of Radioactivity*, and shortly afterwards she was awarded another Nobel Prize, this time in Chemistry.

The Curie couple's eldest daughter followed her parents' careers, continuing research on radioactivity. In the third year of her graduation in Physics and Mathematics at the Sorbonne the Great War broke out and she interrupted her studies to help her mother as radiological nurse in the battlefront. She resumed her post-war studies and pursued her doctorate without difficulty, because she was exceptionally talented. After publishing a study on polonium alpha rays, he began dating Frédéric Joliot, of whom she was a laboratory instructor.

Irene and Frédéric got married and since then their research has always been in partnership. In 1935 they won the Nobel Prize in Chemistry for the discovery of artificial radioisotopes by bombarding alpha particles with nuclei of elements such as magnesium and boron. In their research they obtained more than 400 new radioisotopes. An isotope is an element that occupies the same place in the table (isotope = "same place") as a given element, but with an altered nucleus, with a different amount of neutrons, and therefore with a different mass than that of the original element. For example, by adding neutrons to the aluminum nucleus, we have a new isotope of the same aluminum element. A radioisotope is obviously an isotope that is obtained by radiation. The neutron, as part of the nucleus of the atom, next to the proton, had been discovered earlier by Ernest

Rutherford.

The Joliot-Curie couple left legacy not only in science, but also in political participation, with its anti-fascist militancy. Irene was arrested for having helped, with fundraising, Spanish Republicans fleeing the Franco's dictatorship. When the Nazi occupation of France took place she packed and hid her recent research, so that the Germans did not use that knowledge in the war. It was only in 1949 that she revealed the content of those studies. He died in 1956 by leukemia.

In 1938, in the same decade in which the Joliot-Curie couple received the Nobel, another pair, Otto Hahn and Fritz Strassmann, discovered in Berlin the possibility of fission of the atom. As it is known that it is possible to add neutrons to the nucleus of the atom, forming new isotopes, what they have shown is that we can break the nucleus, generating nuclear energy, or atomic energy. Exiled in Sweden, Lise Meitner and her nephew Otto Frisch gave practical demonstrations of nuclear fission, observing irradiation of uranium with neutrons. Otto Hahn, however, received the Nobel Prize for Chemistry alone in 1944 for the discovery of nuclear fission, since in his writings there was no mention of the role of Lise Meitner, who turned nuclear energy into a practical rather than a theoretical possibility. From a young age she embraced the Lutheran religion, but, nevertheless, she was expelled from Nazi Germany, once she was of Jewish family. He died at the age of 89, in 1968, in Cambridge, England. Unlike other pioneers, she did not develop cancer, because, aware of the risks of the job, she worked very carefully, insisting, for example, with her lab colleagues, that they wash their hands several times a day, never leaving residues in their bodies.

It was on the basis of Lise Meitner's experiments, explained in New York at a conference by Niels Bohr, in 1939, that Enrico Fermi set up the first nuclear reactor, in Chicago, in 1942, after developing the method of bombarding the uranium nucleus with heavy water, what led to the creation of the atomic bomb. Also the use of radioactive isotopes in medicine owes much to it. Fermi had exchanged Italy for the United States shortly after receiving the Nobel Prize in Physics, in 1938, once he was married to a Jewess and

Mussolini had also started there the policy of persecution of the Jews in agreement with Hitler. One of the awards that Lise Meitner won in life was precisely the Enrico Fermi Award.

Radioactivity, as it is well known, has been used in hospitals to heal many ailments. It is a medicine and the medicine works depending on the dosage. The dose is increased and there is a poison, in the vast majority of cases.

The atomic bomb, whose principle is based on the chain reaction of the result of the nucleus bombardment of radioactive element, already showed its capacity of destruction.

Einstein wrote ("Ideas and Opinions"):

*"I do not believe that civilization will be wiped out in a war fought with the atomic bomb. Perhaps two-thirds of the people of the Earth might be killed, but enough men capable of thinking, and enough books, would be left to start again, and civilization could be restored."*

Of course, since the secret of the atomic bomb was with the United States, which shared it with Britain, Einstein proposed that they invite the Russians to form a world government along with the other countries. The text was written in 1945 and in October of that year the United Nations (UN) was established officially in New York. It is not the world government yet, because it does not have a Constitution, nor does it elect a chief of State. It consists of an Assembly of Representatives, a Secretary-General and a Security Council, made up of five fixed representatives, which are United States, England, France, Russia and China, accompanied by ten other countries which occupy the seats in rotation and are chosen from among all the associated nations, which are currently 193. Under the governance of the general secretariat there are various bodies, such as Unesco (science and education), ILO (labor), WTO (trade) and so on, with the role that in national governments is performed by ministries. It also has international courts.

World peace will be secured when the world government is formed, according to Einstein's proposal and desire, provided certain requirements are secured. As the structure already exists, configured at the UN, it is only necessary to have a chief of State, of short term, preferably annual, with an honorary function, such as the English chief of State in relation to Great Britain. There should not be a world Constitution, because it surely would clash with national grand laws. The secretary general then works as world premier. As one of the first measures, one must create the international currency, of the World Bank, always virtual, without printed form. However, there will be an inexorable disaster if, first, a long-term mandate is allowed to this chief of State, and, secondly, if his official and effective residence during the term is installed in capital that has no historical status of national capital and world influence. New York, although it serves to house the premier, does not serve to house the chief of State, because it has no secular history of national capital, as it does with Paris, London, Rome, Tokyo or Washington. The first experience of world presidential residency needs to be done with Paris (otherwise, it will dilute its national seat status in the year 2130, absorbed as regional capital by the European Union, which will be a great loss). If in the course of an eight-year period something injurious befalls the world economy by virtue of that arrangement, then the president is installed in Washington, near the President of the United States.

It should be borne in mind that tyranny is the political model of the time of long-time rulers, intrinsically bellicose, before anything else, and this is contrary to republican citizen life. And the other point is to check the economic woes that nations have suffered throughout history whenever they have installed their maximum leadership in capital without secular historical status. Egypt with Aton, Roman Empire with Ravenna, France with Versailles and Germany with Weimar are just a few examples. Many countries resisted the introduction of new capital until maturation, but at a cost that only complete ignorance of the problem warranted.

Knowing beforehand the possibility of harm, one should avoid reckless experiences with society. In many situations the weight to be borne exceeds the time when the error was present, as observed in the *hysteresis* phenomenon. By this fact of Physics, even after the cause of a certain occurrence ceases, it can continue for some period, as when the electricity that fed an electromagnet is turned off and the magnetization remains for a few minutes. An economy that experiences severe inflation can, even with the elimination of the basic cause, continue with inflationary practice, something that has been called inertial inflation. And to resume the rhythm and culture prior to such a social pathology, not only individuals, but the whole society needs to be endowed with *resilience*, which is the ability of certain metals, such as steel, to vote for the original aspect after subjected to a deformation. People and societies, however, are not naturally resilient. In humans this depends on education, as scientific as in the financial, moral, religious, corporeal and artistic fields.

**Relativity**. The first article on Relativity emerged as a chapter in Jules-Henri Poincaré's book "Science and Method", in 1897, the year following the discovery of Radioactivity, by Becquerel. The article was entitled "The Relativity of Space", and dealt with the possibility of synchronizing clocks.

Graduated in the Polytechnic School of Paris, Poincaré was a graduate in Mathematics and Mining Engineering. Guided by Charles Hermite, he defended his PhD thesis in Mathematics in the year 1879, presenting a new method of solving differential equations. When he died in 1912, the academic world realized that he was the last researcher in history to dominate all of the areas of Mathematics, given the great number of topics and the enormous volume of knowledge that this science had already accumulated at the beginning of the twentieth century.

The conception of the Theory of Relativity did not fall from the sky into the hands of Poincaré, but arose from a practical activity in which he was involved. In 1893 he became a member of the *Bureau des Longitudes*, an agency charged with standardizing time measurement systems for use in maritime navigation, geodesy and astronomy. In 1897 he defended the adoption of a decimal system for measuring hours, instead of the old sexagesimal system, of Assyrian origin, which divides the hour into 60 minutes and the minute into 60 seconds. The proposal was not accepted, but the studies he did to substantiate it suggested the creation of the new theory. Clocks at rest in various places on Earth marked hours at different speeds, relative to the absolute space. They would have to be synchronized, and for this Poincaré developed equations that should solve the problem. It departed from the Woldemar Voigt's concept of local time, judging it to be from Lorentz, and using Lorentz's equations concluded that simultaneity in clocks could be established by convention. In discussing the postulate of the speed of light, he formulated the Principle of Relativity: there is no experiment, mechanic or electromagnetic, that makes it possible to distinguish between a state of uniform motion and a state of rest.

The mathematical development of these ideas Poincaré did in the article "The Theory of Lorentz and the principle of reaction" (*La théorie de Lorentz et le principe de réaction*), 1900. He showed that according to Maxwell-Lorentz's theory, the flux of radiation in a given direction has density equivalent to the value of $e/c^2$, being **e** the energy density and **c** the speed of light. To this "flux density" is that Einstein interpreted as the mass **m**, equivalent to $E/c^2$, in the formula of the Theory of Relativity, which equals the energy **E** to the product $m*c^2$, which has become the most commented equation in the world.

In 1905 Einstein published a series of articles, on various subjects of Physics, and one of them, the one of greater repercussion, came to be the one of name "Theory of the Special Relativity". The Special Relativity, developed by Einstein in this text, is also called Restricted Relativity, once it is applied only to the case in which the curvature of space-time due to gravity has negligible value. Later, in the year 1915, Einstein published the article "Theory of General Relativity", this time as a theory of the gravitational field.

According to the Special Theory of Relativity, the velocity of light in the vacuum is equal in any inertial reference system and in it is reaffirmed the principle of inertia of Galileo, included in Newton's Laws of Dynamics. The equations used in the article brought interpretations that ranged from common sense, such as time dilation, speed limit, and equivalence between mass and energy. As for the latter, Poincaré explained that in Einstein's work it is a mathematical convenience. In fact, the sizing of the two limbs of the equation leads to the same result, which means that they are mathematically equal things, albeit of a different nature.

The two basic postulates of Special Relativity state that (a) there is no privileged referential system, once the physical laws are the same for any referential system, and (b) the velocity of light in the vacuum is a universal constant, independent of the motion of light source. The speed of light is the maximum speed in the universe, and cannot be surpassed by the speed of any other particle. One consequence of the theory is that the time interval between two events, as well as the distance between them, is relative to the observer.

Einstein's conclusions on the speed of light eliminated once and for all the possibility of the existence of the ether, the invisible universal substance upon which the stars sailed, according to an ancient belief. In 1887 the researchers Albert Abraham Michelson and Edward Morley created in the United States a device that tried to prove the nonexistence of the ether, in what was known like the "experiment of Michelson-Morley". The device was called an interferometer and consisted of one piece fitted with a semi-silvered mirror, a semi-mirror, which would divide the monochromatic light into two different angles. The goal was to make the reflection, going in different directions, when coming back, would come at different times if they had to cross the ether. The two beams of light, however, returned at the same instant. Poincaré continued to believe in ether, but Einstein gave credit to the Michelson-Morley experiment, and developed the Special Theory of Relativity on the assumption that ether does not exist. Michelson received the Nobel Prize in Physics in 1907.

As for General Relativity, it is taken into account only in the situations in which the curvature of space-time has to be considered by the effect of the force of gravity. This fact, the curvature of space-time, was proven experimentally in 1919 by the English physicist Arthur Stanley Eddington, through photographs of an eclipse of the Sun that he obtained in Sao Tome and Principe, Africa. Eddington also demonstrated that the transport of energy inside the stars occurs by radiation and convection.

The theory of relativity is nowadays applied in various activities, such as the use of electromagnets, GPS, cathode ray tube of old TVs and the explanation of why metallic mercury is liquid.

Taking into account the results of General Relativity, hundreds of devices are sent to space with the goal of helping to decipher the cosmos, such as the Cassini Probe, the Huygens Probe and the Hubble Telescope, among others. Many facts predicted by Einstein have been proven in the observations made by these devices. One of them, of enormous importance for the cosmology, is the one that shows that the universe is in constant expansion. Einstein, in concluding this, through equations, was reluctant to accept, for he believed that the universe had a fixed size. Currently, data from the Hubble Telescope confirm that the universe expands.

**Quantum**. After the various advances in the late nineteenth century, with the discoveries of X-rays through electron discharge, the composition of the nucleus of the atom with its protons and neutrons, the initial formulation of Relativity Theory, radioactivity, artificial creation of isotopes, nuclear fission and techniques of exploration of nuclear energy in power plants, propulsion engines, radiotherapy and armaments, a formulation appeared in 1900 that more than a century later sounds like a recent thing and, for many, still mysterious, maintaining its characteristic of revolutionary work: Quantum Mechanics.

The word "quantum" comes from Latin, and means "portion", "quantity", "how much".

The initial mark of Quantum Mechanics came in 1900, when German physicist and mathematician Max Karl Ernst Ludwig Planck discovered the constant used to calculate the energy generated by a photon, which is the unit in which light is divided. Planck realized that the light energy is proportional to the radiation frequency, represented by the Greek letter $\nu$ (ni), which led him to deduce that the energy E is given by the product h*$\nu$, where **h** is the value that became known as the *Planck constant*, which has a value of $6.626*10^{-34}$ J*s.

In 1901 he formulated what is now known as Planck's Law, to explain the *radiance*, radiation spectrum of the blackbody. This is an object hypothetically designed in 1862 by Gustav Kirchhoff, a former professor of Planck at the Friedich-Wilhelms University, in Berlin, where Planck continued his university studies started at the University of Munich. A black body absorbs whatever electromagnetic radiation it receives and cannot be crossed by light, nor can reflect it. But unlike what is now known as "dark matter", the blackbody emits radiation, and this is the subject of Planck's research.

Measurements on the blackbody spectrum showed that for a given wavelength a maximum intensity was obtained, whereas for wavelengths above or below that value the intensity only decreased. This was not the expected behavior of the electromagnetic wave, according to Classical Mechanics. The only output for Planck was to postulate that the energy was made by "packets", by discrete particles, not by continuous flow.

These and other contributions to science gave Planck the Nobel Prize for Physics in 1918. But this work was only the beginning of the studies, with formulations and discoveries, of this vast area of knowledge that is the Quantum Theory.

Contrary to common sense, advances in scientific research, while accumulating an immense amount of new knowledge each day, result in simplification of understanding, not complication. Quantum Mechanics, for example, had the role of revealing to scholars that the operation of energy is much simpler than previously one thought.

The adjective "quantum" in the name of this field of study was adopted because the great discovery in the area is that energy does not travel continuously, but in discrete quantities, which are the quanta. Although the set always shows continuity, each quantum of energy is an isolated unit, and the discovery of this fact opened a wide frontier for understandings and uses of energy issues.

When Albert Einstein studied the *photoelectric effect* at the beginning of the twentieth century, including the results in his famous articles of the so-called "annus mirabilis" of 1905, he convinced himself that photons, the elements of electromagnetic radiation, usually light, which caused the effect were emitted as particles (for comparison, the "annus mirabilis" of Isaac Newton was 1666). The photoelectric effect, whose decipherment awarded the Nobel Prize for Physics to Einstein in 1921, was discovered by Heinrich Hertz at the end of the nineteenth century. By the middle of that century, James Clarck Maxwell had discovered that the light wave is electromagnetic. When we apply light, or other type of electromagnetic wave, on a metallic surface, atoms of this surface lose electrons, so that the surface receives energy from the wave through the photons.

Since Christiaan Huygens, a seventeenth-century Dutch mathematician, follower and continuer of Descartes and Galileo's work, wrote that light propagates in waveform, scientists have been advocating this point of view. Isaac Newton discovered decades later that light is transmitted by particles. The controversial particle-wave settled among the researchers, and for all of Newton's weight the scale was weighing heavily on the side of wave propagation advocates. So much so that Hertz understood that the wave itself is the one that energized the surface. Einstein then discovered that elements contained in the wave, the photons, were what produced the phenomenon, not the wave as a whole. Finally, Einstein was able to prove in practice Newton's idea of particle propagation, and at the same time established the conciliation between the polemicists, for he recognized that light is transmitted by waves, i. e., light is particle and it is wave. Both teams were right.

After graduating in Physics from the Federal Institute of Technology in Zurich, Einstein visited several colleges looking for a vacancy to teach, without finding. After two years of searching, a friend offered him a place in the patent office in Switzerland. His job was to analyze the validity of the required patents. Living there with the state of the art of the application of recent scientific ideas by the hand of the Swiss inventors, Einstein acquired a practical sense of the use of science that the scholars of his day did not possess. Thus, while seeing a photon as a *quantum* in the explanation of the photoelectric effect, he aroused in Planck the perception that he would have a great collaborator and a continuer of his researches.

While obtaining his doctorate at the University of Zurich in 1905, the following year he taught at the University of Bern. After passing by several research and teaching centers, in 1914 he yielded to Plank's insistence and went to work in his native Germany, as director of the Kaiser Wilhelm Institute of Physics, acting there until the rise of Nazism in 1932.

In 1913, Niels Bohr, a Danish physicist, applied quantum theory to solve a problem that had been puzzling researchers for decades.

By Rutherford's atomic model, electrons, which revolve around the nucleus, would tend to lose energy and momentum, reducing the radius of their orbit and ultimately falling into the nucleus, blending into protons and neutrons. This, however, did not occur, and no one knew why.

By the model proposed by Bohr, the electrons occupy stable and discrete orbits around the nucleus, without dissipating energy, because each orbit corresponds an electron with its quantified charge. An electron, in order to orbit, needs to be endowed with a minimal discrete amount of energy, below which it would fall. The electron, however, can change its orbit. If it descends from a given orbit to an inner one, it emits a photon. It can also receive a photon and jump to outer, or higher, orbit, if the energy of that photon was equal to the energy difference between the two orbits in question.

Deepening the Bohr model, Werner Heisenberg, Max Born, and Ernest Pascual Jordan, a trio of German physicists, developed a numerical matrix representation system to explain the energy, position, and momentum of the electron in orbits.

From 1924 to 1927 Heisenberg was Bohr's assistant at the University of Copenhagen as a Fellow of the Rockefeller Foundation. He then returned to Germany, where he held various university positions, including that of director of the Kaiser Wilhelm Institute of Physics, now called the Max Planck Institute of Physics. Heisenberg died in Munich in 1976. It has not been ascertained to this day whether this work of Heisenberg in Germany going through the whole period of Nazism aimed at a collaboration with the regime or, on the contrary, a position of resistance.

In 1932 he was awarded the Nobel Prize for Physics, which may have given him an aura of untouchability in front of the agents of the dictatorial government.

In 1915 the French physicist Augustin-Jean Fresnel discovered that the electromagnetic wave, including certainly the wave of light, propagates in different planes. The light wave has an electrical component and, in concomitant motion, a magnetic component, at 90° from the first. Light can be traversed through certain substances that cause it to propagate in a single plane, and there we have the phenomenon of polarization of light. And so that one does not think that only commoners contribute to the development of science, Quantum Mechanics relies on the work of the seventh Duke of Broglie, Prince Louis-Victor Pierre Raymond de Broglie, who migrated from the area of History to Physics and, in the in 1924, in his doctoral thesis, retaking the ideas of Planck and Einstein, showed that the electron itself has undulatory behavior. It was he who finally eliminated the remaining doubts about wave-particle duality. The research of Louis de Broglie made possible the construction of electronic microscopes. De Broglie became a professor at the Henri Poincaré Institute at the University of Paris in 1928, teaching there until 1962, and was awarded the Nobel Prize for Physics in 1929.

In 1927 Heisenberg developed one of the most famous and controversial points of Quantum Theory, the Principle of Uncertainty, according to which it is impossible to accurately measure the linear momentum (velocity) and the position of an electron. In this field, the instrument of labor would therefore have to be the probability. Einstein did not endorse the finding, and stated that "God does not play dice with the world".

Is this set of observable facts determined or indeterminate? To illustrate the case, the Austrian physicist Erwin Schroedinger drew a situation in 1935 that came to be called the "Schroedinger paradox" or "Schroedinger's cat". In an opaque box it is installed a bottle with poisonous gas and also a device containing a radioactive particle with probability of 50% of disintegrating in a given time. If the particle disintegrates, the poisonous gas is released. He puts a cat inside and seals the box. After that expected time, the observer, who is out of the box, does not know if the particle has disintegrated or not, therefore does not know if the cat is alive or not. Without permission to open the box and check, the result of the experiment is that the cat is alive and dead at the same time. Obviously, if the observer could open the box, he would know if the cat died or not.

From this hypothetical cat, and attempts at interpretation to the event, it is that almost all the mysteries and illusions associated with Quantum Mechanics arose, without this being the intention of Schroedinger. There are several possible readings, but three of them stand out. The first is the "Copenhagen interpretation". According to it, the act of opening the box modifies the state of the system. And what we observe now is a cat that has died or is still alive. There is, therefore, a *collapse of the wave function*, irreversible, that renders the measure impaired. Another important view is of the physicist Hugh Everett, who in 1957 launched in the United States the "interpretation of many worlds", which became better known as the case of the "parallel realities". This interpretation postulates a branching of the wave function, for which there are two distinct worlds, one in which the cat is alive, another in which the cat is dead.

Finally, the third stream from this source of ideas is the "interpretation of the objective collapse", according to which the superposition of states is destroyed at the moment the box is opened. With such destruction, there are no parallel worlds. And also because of this destruction, the Copenhagen interpretation is only a hypothesis built for the specific case.

Quantum Mechanics, which deals with the behavior of the particles in the atom, it brought to the laboratory table, at the hands of Planck and Einstein, the valuable information that energy transfers into tiny discrete portions, the quanta, and this allowed advancement of technology in diverse applications. With Quantum Physics it was possible to create the transistor, which replaced the old valve and allowed the miniaturization of numerous devices. With it also it was possible to develop the Internet and GPS, which, as we have seen, also uses the Theory of Relativity. Also Medicine, which uses radioactivity, gained new possibilities with the use of Quantum Mechanics.

The Economics also underwent a major renovation from John Maynard Keynes's book General Theory of Employment, Interest and Money, published in February 1936. One of the main foundations of this work, which replaced the old Political Economy by Macroeconomics, is the idea of uncertainty, inspired by the Heisenberg Principle of Uncertainty. From the understanding adopted by Keynes, a researcher at the University of Cambridge, England, it does not make much sense to invest in long-term economic policies. Keynes and his colleagues sought to point out ways to reduce uncertainty in the short and medium term, demonstrating, for example, that in the laissez-faire market the equilibrium occurs only on special occasions, what requires governments to formulate countercyclical policies to ensure full employment. After Keynes's death in 1946, political activists who were not very keen on change came to treat the idea of "countercyclical policies" as a proposal for "intervention" in the market, thus discouraging governments from adhering to the implicit results of that English economist's work.

**Branes**. In the times of Poincaré, Planck and Einstein, mathematicians already used in the vector spaces elements of numerous dimensions, but in the physical world what was achieved was to pass from the three Euclidean dimensions, which are width, length and height, to four dimensions, by adding the variable time. More recently, in an attempt to explain certain phenomena of string theory, the M Theory (with **M** for membrane) has been developed, according to which, although our senses only account for four dimensions, with which we have become accustomed throughout the twentieth century, there are in fact 11 physical dimensions, in envelopes called branes, or p-branes, which contain more particular forms, called d-branes.

Matter and energy are transmissible only in the space of the first four dimensions, $p + 1$ dimensions, with $p = 3$, where **p** is the number of membranes. Gravity, differently, can pass through the 11 dimensions.

Two options for the shape of the branes are in dispute: they are flat, parallel to each other, or have the shape of hyperbolic paraboloids, i. e., have a saddle shape. For the first case, gravity is distributed between two membranes, in a constant manner. If they are saddle-shaped, there will be areas of greater concentration of the force of gravity, which is reduced as one moves away from the top of the object.

Until 1995 it was considered in superstring theory that a string is a one-dimensional object, like a vibrating line. From then on the strings were included in larger objects, which are the membranes, of two dimensions. For objects of larger dimensions the existence of p-branes was postulated. A string is then defined as a 1-brane object, while a material point is a 0-brane object. Obviously, an object in three-dimensional space is 3-brane type.

The universe in which we act, four dimensions, which are the three spatial coordinates plus the time coordinate, forms a brane, which is immersed in a larger space called bulk, where gravity circulates. These dimensions that transcend the four palpable are contained in an object classified as Calabi-Yau space. Other branes are thought to interact with our fourth-dimensional space, otherwise there would be no reason for anyone to postulate p-branes with **p** greater than 3. Unlike the other forces acting only on our four-dimensional brane, gravity spreads through the other branes, and this fact should explain why it is a weak force.

The cosmology based on M Theory is divided into two currents of thought. One joins the theory the inflationary model (fast expanding universe), while the other works without taking into account that expansionist model.

In 1999 Lisa Randall and Raman Sundrum proposed for brane cosmology what became known as the Randall-Sundrum Model, or RS Model. For this pair of scientists, the universe, beyond our space-time plus one dimension, must be conceived from a warped, or deformed, geometry. We actually live within a five-dimensional universe, but the fundamental particles are confined to the first three, which form a 3-brane. This is what they call TeV brane (Tera electron-volt), or "weak brane". The other brane, within our five-dimensional space, is Plank's brane, or "gravity brane", in which the force of gravity is very intense. The European laboratory LHC (*Large Hadron Collider*) has tried to estimate the measures of strings in one and other brane, studying what happens with the graviton, the hypothetical particle that transmits the gravitational interaction.

For the tendency of inflationary cosmology (the Randall-Sundrum Model serves both tendencies), the universe, or the multiverse, works as an infinitely large ocean in which quantum fluctuations cause the branes to form bubbles, as in boiling water. From time to time, Big Bang moments emerge, which bring down the bubbles and make others appear. There was, therefore, not a single initial Big Bang.

For the contrary tendency, which discards the inflationary

cosmology, everything happens through shocks of branes, which already existed before the Big Bang, and these branes transmit to the universe formed after the shock characteristics that were already in the previous one.

As for d-branes, this letter **d** in the name is a tribute to the mathematician Johannes Dirichlet provided by physicist Joseph Polchinski, co-discoverer of this type of brane in 1989. A d-brane is a p-brane that satisfies the boundary conditions of Dirichlet, on the behavior of liquids in the dynamics of fluids. Polchinski, who died in 2018, was one of the leading theoreticians of superstring theory.

Obviously, it is not up to the high school physics teacher to attempt to teach M Theory to his students, once Basic Mathematics is limited to three-dimensional space when it comes to calculating solids volumes, but it is restricted to the plane, i. e., to the first two dimensions, while regarding algebraic treatment. Thus, the subject branes cannot be something popular. This does not mean that a 16-year-old young cannot study algebra of spaces of four or more dimensions, but there is much to learn before reaching this stage, which will occur in higher education.

Anyway, for those who imagine that hard science stopped in Quantum Mechanics, in the early twentieth century, the superstrings and branes are among us taking sleeping nights of great scholars.

## Chapter 9 - Malthusian overpopulation

**Unemployment**. If a country defeated another in the war and then asked the unsuccessful population if they would prefer to live in unemployment or die, they would almost certainly choose to live in unemployment. If the alternatives were to live in slavery or live in unemployment, with no income, it would almost certainly prefer slavery. In this old system, which should not be confused with the still existing model of servile labor, the worker is legitimate property of some master. When a society abolished slave labor, the prospect was to switch from this system of production to that of wage labor. There is certainly a portion of these economic agents who give themselves to entrepreneurship because they cannot or will not accept being employed by others. But there is no entrepreneurship at all if there are no people employed, forming a buyer market.

As is well known, an intermediate system between slave labor and wage labor was the regime of vassalage, but this was not a world rule and, moreover, was part of a specific and closed period of history.

The above paragraphs seek to argue that only early death - or perhaps some sort of servile or slave life under constant sexual abuse - may be worse than the general unemployment regime. In slavery the worker takes beating and does not exercise any citizenship, but is guaranteed food and clothing. In the system of wage labor, the individual, when employed or retired, is a citizen: he eats, buys his clothes, pays for his housing, and moreover he studies, votes, cares for his children, finances his own leisure, travels, rests. In this same system, being unemployed, without being a rentier or businessman, he is a lump of citizen, because he votes, but he cannot take care of his children, nor to travel, nor to rest, nor to live well, nor to buy clothes, and when he eats it is through donation, whether by the parish, the public service or friends. The exit for some is the practice of crimes, in which they risk life and freedom.

**Malthus**. It underlies the work of Keynes, who draws the initial model of the system of full employment in the market economy, the incompatibility of the market equilibrium with the uncontrolled growth of the world population. Without adequate birth control there is no sustainability for humanity to survive. The first professor of Economics in history, Thomas Robert Malthus, the great inspirer of Keynes's intellectual work, was the first to write a book whose central concern was the problem of the possibility of overpopulation. It is the volume "Essay on the Principle of Population", 1798, a work poorly understood not only at the time of launch, but still at the beginning of the 21$^{st}$ century.

Before Malthus there were important demographers, the first of whom was the seventeenth century English trader John Graunt, who became known for his statistical work in developing his Life Table, which tabulated the probability of death for each age group. She also found, statistically, that for every 1,000 girls, 1,068 boys were born. He is considered the founder of Epidemiology. Another great epidemiologist, quoted by Malthus and, like the latter, also from the eighteenth century, though older, was the German physician Johann Peter Sussmilch, who presented statistics of child births by the sexes, confirming Graunt's numbers, and deepened further studies mortality.

Malthus's approach, unlike that of epidemiologists, turned to the issue of household livelihoods, represented in food. So much so he knew would cause controversy that the first edition of the book he published anonymously.

Anglican Reverend, he says at the beginning of the book that he enthusiastically supported William Pitt the Younger's first version of the "Poor Law Bill", envisioning government cash assistance to families without financial income, because he saw it as a means of to alleviate the work of the parishes, which until then had been the great center of charity of English society. When the government decided to approve a new version of the bill, amplifying the aid, then, based on observations on the effects of the original law, he decided to write the book.

His conclusion was that the financial benefit to the poor without a counterpart requirement was generating a dysfunction that would cause in the long run a socioeconomic tragedy: large contingents of

English subjects being sustained without producing, and at the same time being financed to increase the number of children, would lead to a collapse in the coexistence between supply and demand.

The solution he presented, which was used by Keynes, who embraced the idea, was: Every individual of working age, and healthy enough to do so, should be provided with an occupation, a job, to guarantee him an income. For the disabled, who cannot carry out productive work, the government must provide maintenance, but in public shelters, where they receive the necessary items for sustenance, not including money.

Several chapters of the book initially contain a stick that Malthus created to mark position, as a formula that could represent the core of his ideas: "The population grows in geometric progression as food grows in arithmetic progression". It is only a phrasing of effect, with no mathematical value, since the author did not present the arithmetical progression step or the geometric progression ratio, and most probably he knew of this failure. The problem is that, since the proposition is very imprecise, it does not serve to summarize the theme that he sought to address. It just gives us a vague idea of the problem. However, out of a book of 19 dense chapters, the phrase is the only one that high school students learn in their courses, all around the world, presented by the Geography teacher. And what has happened in practice is that the advancement of technology applied to food production has helped economic systems to meet the demand for food in the nineteenth, twentieth and twenty-first centuries, under better conditions than before the Industrial Revolution, leading young people to conclude, by mechanical induction, that the exponential curve of human production will not exceed the straight line of food production neither in this century nor in the following to this. Now, quite unlike mathematical induction, mechanical induction ("if it happened the day before, yesterday, today, then it will happen tomorrow") is a trap, a false method of deduction. For the sake of remembrance, the demonstration by mathematical induction, a product of Giuseppe Peano's genius, depends on the progression of natural numbers, never the passage of time.

**Antithesis**. Until this conception of the importance of employment, rather than the unparalleled benefit, was accepted by Keynes more than 13 decades later, Malthus obtained as response to his ideas almost always negative reviews. Some branded *ad hominem* arguments, others pinned phrases out of context trying to show that Malthus' motivation was purely moral, others were launching hard attacks on ideas without bothering to read the book.

These are two currents of thought that have always clashed in history. For the first, there is an ideal we should achieve, following Parmenides and Plato, even though we may not know in advance what the aspect of it will be. The machine of the universe, with its laws interpreted mathematically, represents a sign that this ideal exists. The other current, following Epicurus and Aristotle, firmly believes that events in human society are subject to pure chance. Material necessities are the engine of history, and no important decision is made by an injunction of transcendence, and to say that "Paris is worth a Mass" is merely a game of rhetoric. Forming the poor by sustaining their needs without requiring a counterpart, does not provoke any bias in their way of seeing the world, because what matters is to enjoy the present moment in the best possible way, once tomorrow, when the sun rises, chance will tell us where we will be and what we will be doing. We just have to avoid the kind of pleasure we know that will cause us pain. Such is the belief of this second current.

This ideal that the first current postulates can be a great illusion, and we do not have to be guided by something that we do not know what it is or if it does exist, writes the follower of the second team. In response, the adept of the first current invites his opponent to think about Pascal's Bet.

We do not have to demand that every citizen know how to fly a plane or perform hernia surgery. Thus, the reasoning for following the first or the second current lies with a very small proportion of individuals, who are symbol-makers, a number of people smaller than the one of opinion-formers, who do not need to elaborate ideas, but only propagate them. Those who, by opting for the Platonic-idealistic position, or the Epicurean-Aristotelian position (chance), need to construct their argument. On the contrary, they are outlined among the simple credulous followers, who are almost all human beings (this condition is not a defect but a balm for society, otherwise the opposite would lead to a constant conflict in the popular strata by simple defense of ideas).

For the Epicurean-Aristotelian current, beauty is what the person prefers to enjoy at the moment, once, peremptory, chance can change everything in the following hours, including individual perceptions. The other current, the Parmenides-Platonic, understands that there is something more perennial, once there is a good as teleological landmark, a high point of a path that, known or not, people seek to tread. Hence the beautiful identifies with the good. The question that automatically sets in is: Why is there "la beauté du diable", the beauty of the devil, which enchants so many people? The explanation came from the other stream, from Aristotle's writings: Appearances deceive. Our senses do not always allow the truth to reveal itself to us. We are not free to be deceived if we have not yet been brought up to meet the challenge, as it is well illustrated in Carlo Collodi's Pinocchio story. And as much as we prepare ourselves, we will never be completely exempt from making evaluation mistakes. What we know is that those who have no preparation are in the hands of the smart boys. One should not look for indications that one of the two wings is the good and the other the bad, because both bring their positive contributions to the progress of society.

We see that the very notion of "good" depends on the belief in the existence of the ideal. If there is no ideal of justice and truth, then a completely wrong doctrine, harmful to our descendants, can be installed in the world supported by the propaganda of the beauty and the good it emanates. But if there is, incorporating the perspective of the good, an ideal that people deem meritorious in advance, the pictorial feature that is associated with it will appear as beautiful, even if one or another prejudice tends to impose contrary perception. The option for the existence of the ideal does not conflict with free will, as in the case of what has already been said about premonition, once nobody can be sure of what it is like, and if a person arises saying that he has that certainty, without research support more reliable and scrutinized by rules of refutability, he has to be seen as lunatic, prone to impose some tyrannical regime if it gains political power. The canon of the scientific research, moreover, rests on the notion that absolute certainty cannot be attained.

The line that confronts the Malthus' legacy is obviously the second. What if Malthus, by some trick of the wheel of time, encountered the figure of Epicurus in the 21st century to discuss their respective points of view? What would Epicurus say if Malthus argued that a population of eight billion people, tending to increase soon to 10, 15, 21 billion, will, depending on its attitude, face a period of pain as never before imagined that will lead to terrible decisions about the prospect of continuity of the existence of the human species on Earth? Certainly he, without giving up his adherence to materialism, would rethink this calculation of pain and pleasure.

One should not assume that one side is totally wrong and the other side is totally right. The two modes of approach bring important contributions. If we hire two experts to investigate a crime, the one who starts from subjective (ideological) impressions is much less likely to solve the case than the other who works on materialities. Far from the sphere of idealism, in the stomach world the most auspicious clue is this of the one that met the call of the "Follow the Money" recommendation, in spite of the risk of confusion between academic materialism and vulgar materialism.

Since Charles Darwin, inspired by reading the book of Malthus in passing through the pages in which the author deals with the arduous struggle for subsistence, has transferred the vision of the human situation to the wild species, formulating the concept of natural selection and giving robust academic form to the Theory of Evolution, humanity comes, now with knowledge of the cause, developing mechanisms to dominate and combat the dictates of the weather and the traps that nature presents us with innocent cruelty. Bertrand Russell wrote that this is done with the use of birth control and education. They are certainly the two most powerful instruments against the brutality of natural selection, but there are many other resources that we cannot afford. The full employment proposed by his friend Keynes, the end of nuclear arms proposed by Russell himself in partnership with Einstein (1955), the world government

Einstein proposed, Fleming's penicillin, the Sabin vaccine among all other vaccines, modernized electronic communication, which mankind has not yet learned to use with caution, but which is certainly a valuable instrument of mutual protection, all this, besides several historical tools predating Darwin, is an advance in the distancing from the situation of prey of the natural selection.

Every well-educated economist knows the division between a conservative investor and a bold investor, what implies also knowing the distinction between the wasteful citizen, who spends everything he receives with a speed understood only by him, and the prudent citizen, who is spending what is necessary and keeping part of the income for future needs. This one who guards for the future is rewarded with remuneration in the market if he knows how to invest. The other immediately enjoys everything to which he is entitled, within the recommendation of the "carpe diem", by Horace.

Humankind too, as a conscious being, needs to decide between the two behaviors, spendthrift or cautious. The less cautious mankind, the faster it will contribute to incinerating livelihoods on the planet. And surely, the greater the world population, the more difficult it will be to compromise mankind for caution, since the unrestrained increase in numbers of human beings already represents a distancing from that position.

If humanity, which today is overwhelmingly wasteful, counts only on a small portion achieved by adequate education, accepts to follow leaderships committed to sustainability and obey possible laws protecting the environment, including standards of regulation of human birth, since the man is the most polluting agent, if this is the tendency, we must continue to fear, as always, the risk of destruction, but we can convince the young people that the world must be hopeful.

If the contrary is the case, if the general understanding is that this species that has overcome its predators, lower and higher, can continue to reproduce exponentially and wildly without this impacting sustainability policies, then we cannot ask young people to prepare to ensure comfort to your children and grandchildren, because there will not be such a possibility.

**Zero**. Zero growth, in terms of population, the healthiest demographic situation for the future of the Earth, means reproduction of individuals within the limit of the replacement of the specimens. In a mathematically ideal world, each time a citizen dies, the birth of another is provided.

In practice, everything happens without any trauma if the birth rate is fixed on two children per couple, on average.

In an exercise of imagination, let us follow the story of 20 Roman soldiers who sailed in the ocean and discovered a paradise island, still virgin of the presence of human beings. They decided to settle it, fixing residence in it. To do so, they returned to the Italian peninsula and kidnapped 20 Sabine women, very young.

They formed a population of 40 people there.

After ten years, the then president, Remus Columbus, learned from the Institute of Statistics that the population of the island was 80. He then decided that this number should stabilize, and sent a bill to the parliament, approved shortly thereafter, determining that each couple could have two children at most, once that it was the average number of children at that time.

In practice, almost all couples, with rare exceptions, happened to have two children within the established limit. But the population did not remain in 80 inhabitants. It rose to 90, 100, reaching 150. Why was there no stabilization in 80 people? It was discovered over time that the average life was 80 years and the infant mortality was almost nil. They lived with children, parents, grandparents and great-grandparents. When the first great-great grandchildren appeared, the mortality of the elderly suffered a slight increase, because they were already in the time of the natural departure for the beyond life. It is only from then on that the policy of each pair to generate a maximum of two children has led to zero population growth.

If that same rule of two children at most is applied in an old society with high life expectancy, containing people of all age ranges, the result is zero growth in a few years. Further on, an average of two, rather than a maximum of two, can be established, meaning that if a couple has only one child, another may have three.

**Uncertainty**. Unlike those who bet on the absolute prevalence of chance, Keynesians treat uncertainty as fact, but not as a black hole. Institutions, especially those most consolidated in time and space, are mechanisms for coping with uncertainty. One of them is the remunerated bank account, with a stipulated deadline for withdrawal. If the citizen makes a deposit that guarantees income and can only be moved after six months, for example, he is establishing a contract that will protect him from uncertainties that will occur within that period. No one can have the illusion that will be able to guard against uncertainties, which are divided between the quantifiable and the unpredictable. For the quantifiable we have the use of probability as a tool that helps us daily, but for the rest we have to cross fingers, if we are atheists or agnostics, and pray, if we are religious.

Some "mechanisms against Keynesian uncertainty" can be adopted by governments and citizens. Among them we can identify the ones that follow.

1) *Contracts*. Keynes recognized in the contracts, with deadlines and signatures, the first mechanism.

2) *Culture*. One makes best negotiations where there is culture of respect for agreements.

3) *Routine*. Plane of Airline is safer than chartered or sporadic flights.

4) *Merit*. People who are better evaluated in good competitions offer less risk.

5) *Affiliation*: Someone connected to a large and consolidated institution (party, religion) is more reliable.

6) *Planning*. We travel better with those who have a script and plans.

7) *Prophylaxis*. With prophylaxis, epidemics are restricted to cases of absolute unpredictability.

8) *Information*. It is very worth combating information asymmetry and rumors.

9) *Prevention*. Prevention of accidents should not be neglected, even if there is insurance.

10) *Policy*. The less the nomination depends on play and whim, the greater the guarantee.

What about the world, what kinds of prevention can we take against uncertainties? Many of them have been discussed in this book, in the pages above. Measures linked to sustainability are the ones that are most within our reach. Every businessman wants to make a profit, which is not a sin. But the predatory entrepreneur needs to be restrained. Enlightened entrepreneurs and other citizens need to be alert and close ranks in order not to guarantee profit to the predatory entrepreneur.

The company with social responsibility cannot be seen more as a luxury. It must be the rule. Pollution of water, rivers and soil without seeking to remedy the damage should no longer be seen as a lawful way of making money. Neglecting the need for reforestation, neglecting the well-being of employees, and disregarding the effects of environmental impacts in the vicinity of the factory, all constitute examples of lack of citizenship. Negative externalities are not clouds of rose essence that the weather raises and disperses through the atmosphere. On the contrary, they are signs of misadministration.

A predatory entrepreneur pollutes, destroys nature without recomposing, invests in measures to harm employees, ignores the situation of the children of these ones, deteriorates the market in which he operates, destroys legitimate competition and tricks the tax, even in cases where the rules of taxes are not stupid. One should not expect the education system alone to dilute and neutralize this type of economic agent. The laws are what must inhibit them and take away their space for action, because time is short and nature, brutal and deaf as it is, will never cease to be equally fragile.

We also need to create and strengthen international institutions whose purpose, whether explicit or not, is to reduce uncertainty about the continuity of life on Earth. Nowadays, the main of these entities is the UN, but we can have many others, with different actions. Within the UN itself, in addition to the Climate Panel, it is urgent to create a network of environmental agents, with a legal enforcement role similar to the work of the Ngo Greenpeace. Unicef, for its part, should not continue to collect separate funds from citizens, as if it were an Ngo, but it must be supported by a system of contributions from member governments to the UN cash box.

Absolutist monarchies, dictatorships, and all systems of republics with long-lived presidents, which are false republics, must be abolished from the face of the Earth, not only by pressure from the UN, but by international trade systems and all international exchange schemes.

Nuclear plants around the world should not only be monitored by the UN International Atomic Energy Agency, but should have the UN as co-owners, which can be done through World Bank participations.

And for great achievements, how can we ensure that they are not victims of uncertainty? In the items Prophylaxis and Prevention, our attitude must follow the "paradigm of fire doors". Modern buildings are equipped in their architecture with empty spaces between compartments as fire prevention. To go from room A to room B, the citizen passes through a steel door, which gives access to a door and to another steel door, which leads to the second room. It is possible and necessary to install "fire doors" to preserve democracy, full employment, public education and many other social advances. Without these doors, everything is at the mercy of foreseeable uncertainties and hurricanes.

What are the fire doors to preserve democracy, for example? The first is the strengthening of the *federation*, because any dictator likes to favor the "folklore" of the regions, but not the political powers of these, which are against him. The second door is the establishing of political *term* limit, because a chief of State that in the Republic can exceed ten years in power, two five-year terms, already structures beforehand as a dictator. The third door is to prevent a lower-ranking *military* from reaching the State leadership, because a corporal or even a colonel who compels the generals to salute him is a political depraved, a born coup, and in this field one must also ensure that a general in the State leadership always has as his successor a civilian. The fourth door is the guarantee that the *parliament* is not closed, once it is the privileged vigilance of the ruler, so that parliamentary rules that have the legislative house dissolved when there is no agreement to maintain or form a government need to be reformulated, with the institution of the post of deputy chief, always nominating a vice for the premier who takes office in the government, and also with the adoption of the majority award (the party that wins more seats takes more than half of all seats), with clear tiebreaker criteria when it is the case. The fifth door is the perpetual veto to anyone who has been convicted of attempted *coup* or has been diagnosed and treated as a schizophrenic. Obviously, the number of preventions is not exhausted in these five, but they are the priority. Some mechanisms are already incorporated into the constitutions of many countries, such as the veto as for being a foreigner, an illiterate and an under-aged, generally below 35, an age, however, that should be changed to 49, seven sevens. These and other restrictions need to be consolidated, without neglecting the principle of non-discrimination based on ethnicity, physical fitness, gender, religion and province.

Like democracy, every institution of great value for the health of social life must be protected by efficient "fire doors".

**Challenges**. Many improvements to human life, some already pre-conceived and awaiting technical feasibility, can and should arise if we win the great battle of preserving life. Among them can be remembered those that follow.

1 - *Pluvial.* Control and deciphering of the rain cycle, with the creation of Pluvial Engineering, to end the drought and deserts.

2 - *Sustainability.* Total replacement of fossil fuels by solar energy and renewable energy.

3 - *Employment.* Advent of full employment worldwide.

4 - *Toilets.* Toilet incinerator microwave (end of black water in the sewer).

5 - *Proteins.* Scale production of artificial milk and meat via stem cells, avoiding the emission of methane gas from cattle in the pasture.

6 - *Prevention.* Forecasting volcanoes and earthquakes.

7 - *Teleportation.* Invention of the teleportation system of goods.

8 - *Restoration.* Reconstruction of the organs of the human body

through adult stem cells.

9 - *Teething*. Method of natural restoration of teeth and hair.

10 - *Resuscitation*. Domain of reversal of brain death. Further on, reconstitution of body and animal life from the skeleton via DNA, being careful not to create "Jurassic Park".

**Conclusion**. If it is difficult to know what is good or what is ideal, some of those items that the most conscious people seek to reach leave no doubt that they are located on the side of truth and justice and therefore of good. Examples are: Peace among nations, responsible parenthood, universalization of basic education, care for children, remuneration for all citizens through employment or entrepreneurship, valorization of life through rejection of the forms of programmed death, monetary stability of the country, financial credit, the protection of forests and rivers, correct and humanized law, measures against prejudices, prohibition of manufacture and carrying of short guns (which cowards hide in their coat), absence of tyrannical governments.

In many situations we judge that what we do is right, that we are doing some good to mankind, and we find out from one moment to the other that we were rightly mistaken. This was the case with the bleeding technique, already mentioned, but there are numerous other examples. There are also cases of pitiful negligence that we have committed because we are not yet aware of the seriousness of the act. In this account, we have the disregard for the environment, when we eliminate species for food use, when we polluted water and air at ease, when we carelessly built machines and factories that contributed daily to the increase of global warming, all of these things because we imagined that the natural goods of our surroundings came from elastic and inexhaustible source.

There is evidence today that we make a mistake when we expose our young children to electronic screen devices, and perhaps even to the radio. Some psychiatrists recommend that we avoid leaving children under the age of three years in front of the TV, because this can, in most cases, exert negative interference in language development. And there are those who have observed that children and teenagers making intensive use of smartphones or any computer can indelibly damage the functioning of their natural memory.

To test suspicion it is necessary to follow control groups, what is not difficult, once there are religious communities that do not allow the use of electronic screen devices by children and young people. For example, one can measure the mean time of each of the two groups, what uses cell phone and what does not use, for language acquisition, although there is already evidence that the delay is higher in the electronics group. But it is also possible to measure the natural storage capacity in both groups, to verify if the group without electronics stays healthier, i. e., with sharper memory and greater retention power over time. If the damage is proven, remembering that Sergio Porto, a humorous writer from Rio de Janeiro, called the television "machine for making crazes", we can adapt the nickname for the smartphone and the tablet, calling them "child dumbing machine".

And since we speak in religious communities, we cannot fail to register a very abrupt change, to the standards of behavior with which mankind was accustomed. Since the mid-1980s, with the increasing of the population access to electronic media, the population has been abandoning religion. In the Netherlands, Protestant churches have been severely depleted and have been transformed into libraries, coffee houses and concert halls. In Canada, the same has been happening with Catholic churches. In the United States, there was 90% of the population claiming to be Christians before the Internet was available, with only 80% remaining now. Those 10% of the difference did not change their religion, but they just left it aside. This, it seems, is a path with no return. Churches, Catholic or Protestant, will vouch foolishly if they insist on the return of these old faithful, because the tendency is to "lose" more. However, religious ministers should not make a pessimistic reading of these facts. What must be maintained in Western society is respect for Christian culture. If agnostics embrace this cause, the work of the churches in the preceding centuries will bear fruit. For clerics, the ideal is children being trained in catechism or Sunday school, receiving the teachings that are the founders of our society.

But if these values are kept in the culture and passed on to the new generations, even outside the churches, there will be no cause for great regrets. There will be cause, yes, if happens to exist an arrogant rejection of the humanitarian legacy we inherited from Christianity. The importance of forgiveness (offering the other side), the cultivation of universal brotherhood (Christian charity), recognition of the positive meaning of learning not to shoplift, not to steal, not to kill, not to betray, and not to swear a false witness, if all transmitted by the agnostics to their children, Christian culture will be present in the coming times. It is even better if reading the New Testament becomes a widespread practice in youth. Keynes wrote that the ruler's bedside book should be the New Testament. The recommendation, however, will only have good effects if that ruler is not neophyte in those knowledge.

Catholic clergymen are distressed to see that the learning that children receive in the catechism is soon despised and even ridiculed. This, however, is only a cover, a work whose result does not boast of its own gain. The foundation is in place. The priest must take pity not on his catechumen, but on the young man who disdains catechetical learning without having gone through it, because he can fall into terrifying hands, depending on his social situation. A couple of intellectuals who do not take their young son to the catechism because they think this is a waste of time, once a few years later this son will be denying the lessons he received there, this couple is putting their child at risk. The best way for the boy is to attend catechesis. If he reinterprets all this on his own, which will give the impression of rebellion, then he will be showing the positive product of the work. A Catholic who does not doubt the ancient canons of the Church, especially the seventh-century church, that inspired Prophet Muhammad, is a bad Catholic.

The school of the next times will have to be as efficient as this is possible. Three centuries ago it educated people who would live a few years. From the 21$^{st}$ century onwards, the preparation it gives is for people who will live on average 70, 80, 90 or even more than 100 years. Within another century, longevity may reach somewhere between 200 and 300 years. If the values and internships provided to children by school leave many gaps, the bad service will have repercussions for two centuries or more. The apprenticeships related to religion are in this set. Einstein wrote that the religion teacher would find it difficult to teach children that the deity is an anthropomorphic being, a white-bearded elder, as in the Greek polytheism, as these children acquire scientific knowledge. In fact, that anthropomorphism was the language of 3,000 or 4,000 years ago. In the fourth century, of the bishops Jerome of Stridon and Augustine of Hippo, they were worth the same linguistic images. And they were worth even in the times of Joan of Arc, of the Hundred Years War. After the laboratories of Galileo, Newton, Darwin, Pasteur, Marie Curie, Fermi and Hawking, it becomes necessary to update the speech and texts. Or the totality of what is said about religion, transcendence, and Supreme Being will only continue to make sense before audiences completely oblivious to Descartes' advice, that we must doubt everything.

Living much more than before, every citizen of the third millennium should receive solid education in childhood. And he will be aware that he will take the place of two or three of his ancestors in the world. While a period of 120 years contained the lives of three citizens, decades ago, in a few more decades it will be the lifetime of a single person. If the world has 12 billion people with such longevity, with a life expectancy of 40 years the same world population would be four billion.

With the eight billion of 2018, it is time to take ownership of the understanding that overpopulation of the human species is the most dangerous time bomb for the Earth. Defeating our predators, and thereby ensuring greater longevity, we become the most damaging pest. Hawking certainly lost faith in our ability to stop being a plague. But there is a way to reverse such a diagnosis.

We do not need to decimate our species, as the crew of the sinking boat uses to do, hoping to save some among them. We must boast at four winds that our central path is to reduce the birth rate. The eight million that we are already in the world deserve to enjoy life as best we can. If we simply duplicate this contingent, believing that it is enough to reduce the emission of carbon dioxide, the world will be hopelessly lost. Reducing pollutants by cultivating sustainability is vital, but this is not to insist on the illusion that the plague has come to reproduce itself irrationally and wait for the worst.

In order to plan the welfare of society, since it will not be of great value to stabilize the population by eight million and to maintain a large share of unemployment and misery, it will be necessary to establish the regime of Keynesian full employment. And this plan is only feasible if population growth does not burst budgets. To speak of a "demographic bonus", imagining some gain for having a young majority in a country, is something of an economist with a head of the classical times, not of people versed in Macroeconomics. If we build a dam to store a certain volume of water, an event that brings up twice the expected volume will represent disaster. So is the full employment plan. So is any plan of well-being for society.

We cannot have condescension with the disregard of governments in the implementation of Keynes's full employment plan. Throughout his work it is explicit that the volume of employment is the responsibility of politics, of which the market is hostage. If the government's choice is to let the course of high unemployment run freely, this is a policy. What is known is that within governments, and the party, there are those who make policy of omission and those who make effective policy. In the early years of the 21$^{st}$ century, the primeval dictates is to replace factory jobs and even white-collar by robots. This policy has provoked the biggest wave of migration in the world, with millions of unemployed people crossing the Mediterranean Sea in the north or walking in copious caravans from many poor countries in the Middle East and nearby, such as Pakistan, towards the European Union, what excited the British of the interior to approve the proposal of the "Brexit", the exit of the confederation. If the policy is that of full employment, and not that of uncommitted contemplation, these populations do not exchange their safe livelihood for mortal adventures, as it is the Maghreb's crossing to Europe in precarious and overcrowded vessels. For millennia the population of North Africa has been separated from the southern population by the Sahara Desert, but in the 21$^{st}$ century the ease of transport has broken this barrier, causing all Africa to reach the coast of Libya and Algeria, and cross the sea.

Companies necessarily pay taxes, and they pay for one of those two policies. The more advantageous of the two is undoubtedly full employment, which creates a market rather than destroys it, since there is no faster and more secure means of reducing and impoverishing the market than unemployment policy.

The key to reducing the birth rate, efficiently, without cruelty, is in the texts of Aristotle. He wrote that the minimum age for marriage, meaning "cohabitation", should be 35 years-old for the man and 28 years-old for the woman, five sevens and four sevens, respectively. We do not have to be so hard on our young people. The minimum age can be 30 years for men and 28 years for women. The difference in age is not for the reason required by the Stagirite philosopher, that the man should be seven years older for the woman not to command him, but because the woman has fertile age restricted to a much shorter period than the man. Since a man maintains his fertility at age 50, 60, or over, a second marriage with a young woman must curb a second offspring, restraining it to one child. If there is a third marriage, a heavy fine should be instituted in the case of new breeding. With the minimum age of 30 years for the man, there will be children prior to cohabitation, but they will be residual cases, of those raised by the grandparents. And education should be responsible for providing responsible parenting.

Older societies, such as India and China, must urgently institute this Aristotelian restraint, especially now that China has relaxed its one-child policy. India, as we can see by the numbers, surpasses China by population by 2030. Islamic countries will be the most resistant to adopting such practices, but if other cultures, such as Christian and Zen Buddhist, take seriously the purpose of the birth restriction, the Islamists will also realize that growing contingent to suffer and to harm the health of the planet is not a policy to be defended.

Now our task is to invest in sustainability, knowing that we are running against the clock. For the moment, we are not aware of damage caused, for example, by the use of solar energy, which points us a reasonably safe way to replace the uses of fossil fuels. At least ten almost indispensable appliances have solar powered versions: 1) calculator, 2) cell phone, 3) lamp, 4) video camera, 5) shower, 6) kitchen, 7) laptop, 8) car, 9) train, 10) airplane.

*Powered solar train in India*

Clean energy, clean-up, efficient basic education for all, full employment, reforestation, end of atomic weapons, end of long-term presidencies, abolition of wars, democratic governments and birth control, these are our tools to help the planet to stay alive for centuries. And to control the birth rate, avoiding the supreme misfortune of unsustainable overpopulation, the recipe is Aristotle's policy: minimum age for cohabitation imposed by all responsible governments. The public power should never enter the citizen's alcove to supervise this, but must control the norm with rules for the notary public, real estate industry, condominiums, electricity services, water distributors, health posts, and so on. The children of more mature people, contrary to what Aristotle imagined, are not stunted. What they have is a richer and more experienced heritage of life.

@cacildo
cacildomarques@gmail.com